OWN IT!

Building An Accountability-Rich Culture Together

Leta M. Beam

EVERYDAY LEADERSHIP SERIES #2:
ACCOUNTABILITY

HUGO HOUSE PUBLISHERS

Limits of Liability and Disclaimer of Warranty

The author and publisher shall not be liable for your misuse of this material. This book is strictly for informational and educational purposes.

Warning—Disclaimer

The purpose of this book is to educate and entertain. The author and/or publisher do not guarantee that anyone following these techniques, suggestions, tips, ideas, or strategies will become successful. The author and/or publisher shall have neither liability nor responsibility to anyone with respect to any loss or damage caused, or alleged to be caused, directly or indirectly by the information contained in this book.

ISBN: 978-1-936449-98-9

Library of Congress Control Number: 2017936422

Cover Design & Interior Layout: Ronda Taylor, www.RondaTaylor.com

Hugo House Publishers
Denver, Colorado
Austin, Texas
www.HugoHousePublishers.com

Dedication

To the often unsung heroes of workplaces across the world
who are doing the right thing every day.

Contents

PART ONE
SETTING THE STAGE

PART TWO
ACCOUNTABILITY: WHAT IT'S ALL ABOUT

PART THREE
CHOOSE ACCOUNTABILITY TOGETHER!

Raging Appreciation

In their book, *The Power of Appreciation: The Key to a Vibrant Life*, Noelle Nelson and Jeannine Calaba share confirming research that when people feel appreciation, good things happen to their minds, heart, and bodies. But, they go on to assert, appreciation is much more than a feel-good mantra. It is an actual force, an energy that can be harnessed and used to transform our daily life—relationships, work, health and aging, finances, crises, and much more.[1] These two authors put into words what I have unequivocally experienced in my life!

And so, as is my habit, I want to launch this second volume of the Everyday Leadership series by highlighting for you some of the many people to whom I owe a deep debt of gratitude:

- ✪ Shannon Strasser, my daughter and business partner. She not only elevated her game and took increasing responsibility for leading Vantage International to create the space for me to write but also handled early editing of the manuscript, participated in mind-storming sessions for creative solutions and searched for just the right quotes! Most importantly, she encouraged me, tweaked my inner spirit, pushed me through a bout of writer's block and kept me fanatically focused on the importance of the message.

- ✪ Jim Buckheit, my husband and accountability hero. Jim has so many wonderful talents and gifts that I admire. And at the top of the list is his steadfast determination to do what is right—

1   Nelson Noelle, C. Ph.D. and Jeannine Lemare Calaba, Psy.D. *The Power of Appreciation*. Hillsboro, Oregon: Beyond Words Publishing, 2003. Print.

regardless of what others are doing and regardless of the cost. His everyday decisions, whether at home, at work or in our community, continually inspire me and others.

✪ My editor, Dr. Patricia Ross. There's a saying, "Everyone wants to have written a book but nobody wants to write one" Writing a book is tougher than you might think. Writing a second book seems to be even trickier. My partnership with Patricia makes the journey a smoother, more enjoyable one. Our mutual commitment to accountability is no small part of our success equation.

✪ My utterly amazing clients. I am so fortunate to have clients who teach me so much; who role model accountable behavior more often than not; who are hungry to learn and willing to unlearn; and who lift up the timely message of workplace accountability with gusto and verve. This book is a testament to you all!

"Appreciation can make a day, even change a life. Your willingness to put it into words is all that is necessary."

Margaret Cousins

SETTING THE STAGE

OWN IT!: *Building an Accountability-Rich Culture Together*

1

We Started a Movement!

Have you ever wondered if the way we behave toward each other at work and how we approach our actual job is *really* the best that we can be?

It's been quite a few years since I first started to wonder that. At different times, I was either being told what to do and when to do it or telling others what they should be doing. It seemed so wrong-headed to me that most workplace relationships were based firmly on the assumption that most of us could not be trusted to do the right thing on our own! It often felt as though we were never doing it fast enough or good enough or were constantly trying to prove our worth but chronically disappointed in one another no matter what we did.

For the longest time I went along with this unproductive way of thinking and behaving even though it was less and less of a fit for me ethically. Telling someone what to do or being told what to produce was the only work experience that I knew. It felt familiar. It was pretty predictable. And it eventually became a longstanding habit that felt as though it was just the way it was and would always be. It was a thought rut, a pretty rigid expectation of work life. And the truth is that I became darn successful at it.

But somewhere deep inside of me, I knew that there had to be other possibilities. I had, at the time, what I called an itch for occupational adventure. I vowed to find another, more authentic, way of getting important work done together. Despite warnings from mentors, family, friends and other smart people, I simply decided to take the risk of being myself, finding a new leadership groove that was all my own, and co-creating a different workplace experience with like-minded people.

I can trace back my passion for coach leadership and for creating engaging, vibrant organizational cultures to that decision point. It was a *kairos* moment. *Kairos* is one of my favorite words. It's a Greek word, literally meaning God's time. For me, it has come to mean a critical moment in time when opportunity and action intersect. I didn't recognize it then but by that act of stepping outside of what others thought was the "correct" way to work, I *started a movement!*

I began in small ways to work within, on myself, to define and refine (or polish) my own offbeat (I mean that in a positive way!) but wonderful leadership style. I began to think of myself and others differently at work. I asked myself what if we —

- ★ treat each other as capable and well-intended adults
- ★ help each other to learn and grow
- ★ encourage a new level of creativity
- ★ share power and decision making
- ★ genuinely appreciate the contributions and greatness of others, even when it was a very different "brand" than mine?

Because change happens from within, I realized that I had to start on myself. So I then decided to

- ✪ show up for work with a remarkably different mindset and a different set of expectations framed by a focus that many sparks of possibility existed in all situations
- ✪ practice radical hospitality, welcoming others into conversations, mind-storming cross functionally and erring on the side of inclusion rather than exclusion
- ✪ fearlessly begin to find ways to do things differently and better
- ✪ simply have more fun; I decided to enjoy the journey more and obsess on the destination (the outcome) less
- ✪ earnestly choose to connect with the people around me; to trust more and believe more
- ✪ believe that most people want to make a difference through the work that they do.

The results were exactly what I had envisioned. People were more engaged with me; I saw the inklings of them stepping outside of their own comfort zone and following what I did. My new energy went viral!

Most importantly, I realized that the way to sustain a high-performance level was to build strong, healthy adult relationships that helped everyone to understand the meaningful nature of their contributions and their connection to the overall success of the organization. To the best of my ability at the time, I modeled the behavior and approach that was missing from my past experiences.

Once my own transformation was underway, I increasingly focused my energy outward. One conversation at a time, I began to spread an unassuming new message of collective leadership and full-throttle engagement at work. As you might expect, reactions ranged from intrigue to hopefulness, to enthusiasm to skepticism, cynicism and even dismissal. It wasn't until someone shared a TED.com video and insisted that I watch it immediately that I connected a few dots and began to see the potential in those everyday interactions.

The video is affectionately called "Shirtless Dancing Guy" and in true TED Talk form, it delivered a great message in a fun, quirky way. I want you to watch the video, too, so I don't want to be a buzzkill and reveal too much. But I'll give you the big take-away here: dare to think differently and act differently from the crowd. Risk not just being a "lone nut" because that's how you start a movement, but be the first brave follower and get others to follow as well.

That message clicked with me then as it still does now. There were plenty of times when I felt like the "lone nut," but gradually other people joined in. And so, I reframed the experience, and started calling it a *movement*. I also quickly found out that I wasn't really a lone nut; there was a chorus of voices, including thought leaders such as Tom Peters, Warren Bennis, Richard Greenleaf and Dan Pink, delivering the same powerful refrain: the "same-ole, same-ole" way of just being told what to do will not propel us forward. We needed to create a fresh start together.

Gradually, the movement picked up steam. Nineteen years ago, that singular *kairos* moment that I described earlier gave birth to my leadership and business-coaching enterprise, Vantage International. And since then, the movement has reached its tipping point as more and more of us have come to realize that if we want to share a bright future together, we need to forge a different kind of community experience together. And as that insight seeps into our collective consciousness at work, it's becoming what we all know! Hurrah for us!

It became increasingly important for me to document the research, insights, tactics, tools and techniques that helped me get to where I wanted to be. I vividly remember a valued colleague, Izzy, saying to me one day at a leadership conference, "You've been saying these same things (as the presenters at the conference) for years. When are you going to write it all down and give people a roadmap that they can believe in?" A few years ago I did just that; I created the *Everyday Leadership* series when my first book, *Take The Lead*, was published. It was meant to break through the fog of mediocrity that has permanently settled in at many organizations by offering a blueprint for what I call *full-throttle engagement powered by coaching*. What that means is simply this: it is my call to action to all of us to completely overhaul the meaning of leadership in our world of work; to show up leading from our seats day in and day out; to expect the very best from ourselves and others; to see ourselves as powerful forces and to behave accordingly. And while the response to *Take The Lead* has been very rewarding, it's not nearly as gratifying as the powerful realization, that feeling in your gut, that together we're fueling a game-changing movement.

I extend a warm and heartfelt welcome to each of you, my colleagues, as we embark on the second leg of our leadership adventure and tackle head on one of the most crucial (or what I call jugular) elements of contemporary business success—workplace accountability. *Own It!* is the second volume in *The Everyday Leadership* Series. It's intentionally built on the world view, leadership model, and comprehensive skill set found in *Take The Lead*.

Let me be crystal clear on this point: From my perspective, only when we truly understand the changing nature of leadership and its pivotal link to full-throttle engagement at work AND put that new understanding into practice day after day, will we be ready to choose accountability individually and collectively.

I hope that as you read, you will jump on board with the ideas presented here. They are meant to ignite a passion in you to be accountable from within, not rely upon someone else to do that fundamental task for you.

It's not always easy, but the rewards for yourself and your coworkers will make the bumps in the road not only worth it but an intrinsic part of your journey to *own* everything you do.

OWN IT!: *Building an Accountability-Rich Culture Together*

2

The End Game:
A Culture of Owners, Not Renters

Alex is a nice young man. He does good (but not great)
work as a case manager. In other areas, his performance is
pretty uneven. He is regularly tardy; calls in "sick" frequently
and at the last minute; and has a habit of taking extended
lunches and breaks. Others have noticed this pattern. Some,
including his boss, Jerry, look the other way, because he's
such a nice guy.

Most of us know someone like this. They "phone it in," and drive the
rest of us crazy because everyone else is left picking up the pieces to make
sure his work gets done. We would all rather work with someone like this:

Karen is an administrative assistant. As she and I walked
together through her department, she stopped frequently to
give directions to several lost clients. She picked up trash,
straightened up chairs, and greeted her colleagues across the
organization by name. I just knew she was a joy to work with,
making sure her work was done well and, at the same time,
helping others so that everyone around her was successful.

What's the difference? Karen is engaged, cares about her work, her
teammates, everything about what she does. Alex, not so much.

Karen is "leading from her seat," an expression from *Take the Lead*,
which means she has taken on the responsibility to be the very best administrative assistant she can be. She is admired, listened to, and her coworkers
accept her help. She gets the long-term vision of what it might be like if we

all showed up as our best selves each day. And she also intrinsically operates from something even more fundamental. She understands what it means to be an owner.

A Fundamental Difference

Several years ago, I was facilitating an educational program when someone asked me a question about how you get someone to be fully accountable for their work. Instead of answering her outright, I asked her this provocative question: *What's the difference between someone who owns their home and rents it?*

This analogy is not intended as a "put down" to owners, renters or landlords. I have owned my own home, rented my home, and I have been a landlord, and I sincerely believe that an owner has a different attitude or mindset about their home than someone who is renting. (Do you agree with me?)

I often ask individuals or groups to note the difference between the two: owners and renters. I had this audience jot down some thoughts on what an owner might think or feel about her/his property.

I invite you to do that now:

_____

_____

_____

_____

Now, do the same thing for the renter:

_____

_____

_____

_____

I then had everyone compare notes. Here are some of the sentiments that I think owners often have:

"I'm proud of my property! The way that I maintain and enhance this home is a reflection on me"

"Everything that I do creates more value in the property."

"If something needs attention, it's on me to get that done."

"I'm in this for the long haul."

And these are some of the ways that renters may think:

"I'll do what I'm obligated to do in my renter's agreement (contract), but not a whole lot more."

"I'm not going to live here forever, so I'm not going to improve things too much. After all, what would I get out of it?"

"If something goes wrong, I'm not responsible. It's the owner's problem to handle. I have his number programmed into my phone."

It's not hard to see where I'm going with this. Working in the "same-old same-old" pattern of boss/employee creates a culture of renters. A person taking responsibility not only for their own position but for the overall well-being of entire organization is an *owner.*

Let's revisit the two people with whom I started this chapter. Karen, the conscientious administrative assistant "owns" her work. Alex, the case manager, is a renter and unfortunately a fairly poor one at that.

Alex is just doing his j-o-b so he can get his paycheck. He's unhappy, and it shows. Karen gets that

leading from your seat, coaching others around you and achieving full throttle engagement is the power and freedom that comes from being an "owner" of the organization.

What she does every day at work is more than a "j-o-b": it fulfills her, she has purpose, and she elevates those around her as well.

For several years, I have successfully used this renter/owner analogy to stimulate debate and dialogue with clients and audiences. Sometimes I'm challenged. Once, some astute attendee expanded the analogy even further by asking, "What about a rent-to-own mindset?" I had to give that one a little thought, but I loved the insight and the challenge! So what would the renter-to-owner be thinking?

"I'm taking it one step at a time but someday soon, this will be my property."

"Now I've got some skin in the game. Things are different. I've got to step up and think about the future."

I would suggest, in other words, that "renting to own" is like a temporary job that may go permanent. If you're acting like an owner, well then you are one!

This analogy should be pretty obvious. It's the foundational idea of workplace accountability. At its core, a fully accountable culture is full of owners rather than renters!

The Self-Employed Mindset

Here's another way to look at the idea of accountability. Ask anyone you know who is self-employed how much they care about their work and how passionate they are about providing their customers with an exceptional experience. They believe wholeheartedly in their vision and mission; their behavior and choices are aligned with their values. They do the right thing and deliver what they promise; otherwise, their company will not be around very long. They literally own their business.

In his book, *We Are All Self Employed*, Cliff Hakim argues that

> Workers eventually came to believe that those who owned their own companies were self-employed and those who worked for organizations were entitled to their job, benefits, and perks. They were not, however, self-employed.

The urgent message of *We Are All Self-Employed* is that the "employed" attitude no longer serves anyone well. In fact, it is increasingly hamstringing our success together. A "self-employed" attitude has "emerged as the central belief for fueling your work life."[2]

I believe that when anyone in any organization "owns it," there is a wonderful opportunity to shift from "renter" to "owner," which is akin to shifting from an "employed" to a "self-employed" mindset.

---

2   Hakim, Cliff. We Are All Self-Employed: How to Take Control of Your Career. San Francisco, California: Berrett-Koehler Publishers, Inc, 2003. Print.

Today, I believe that this shift in thinking and behaving is our 911 call to action.

To be accountable is to see oneself as self-employed and act as an owner. What can you create with that mindset? That is another coaching question I invite you to answer. To start, let's do a quick "mind storming" exercise. It is engaging not just our brain but our minds.

Let's consider the different approaches of someone who views her/himself as an owner at work versus someone who views her/himself as *just an* employee.

I'm an OWNER	I'm just an employee
Go the extra mile	Do what's asked/expected
Always follow rules, policies, procedures	Usually follow rules, policy
Interested in finding better ways to work	Not all that motivated to improve
Active & creative problem solver	Reluctant problem solver/Waits for others to provide the fix
Generally upbeat w/'can do' attitude	Attitude is dependent on others/situations
Almost always part of solution	Sometimes part of the problem
Dedicated, committed (all in)	Provisionally committed
Work to see the bigger picture	Focus on j-o-b duties
The buck stops here	"Not my responsibility"
We're on in this together	What's in it for me?
I'm important to the success of my organization	Does what I do each day matter?
Love to learn & grow	Will learn & grow if necessary
Coach self & others	Accept coaching (maybe)
I'm proud to work here	This is a good as any place
Do the right thing	Do the easy thing
Take an active role	Take a more passive role
Choose a winning attitude	Choose a whining attitude

Now it's your turn. Which are you most days? Do you have a "self-employed" or owner's approach to your work day? Or do you see yourself as "just an employee" with a "renter's" attitude? Jot down any insights that you have here:

(NOTE: This is a free-form, no "wrong-answer" zone. Write whatever comes to mind—there is no right or wrong to this and no one need look at it but you. This is a hands-on learning experience, so this is the time for you to pause a moment and gather your thoughts about what you've just read. This is something I will ask you to do periodically throughout the book.)

_____

_____

_____

_____

_____

_____

_____

And finally: How would your organization be better and different if you began to think and act as an owner?

_____

_____

_____

_____

_____

_____

_____

"You are bigger than your defined role and you are much more than your job title. Play your part...transcend your job title. BE A HERO."

Luke Bucklin
Sierra Bravo Corporation

Who's In Charge of the Success of This Place?

I hope the foundational idea behind *Own It!* is now pretty clear. In order for us to continue to succeed at work, we must all foster an environment in which more and more of us see ourselves as owners. In small ways and large, we're cultivating a culture full of owners, and not simply owning our individual j-o-b duties either. That's not nearly great enough! Each of us must be committed, both head and heart, to the success of the entire organization and act accordingly. This is what accountability is all about.

In this regard, we need to act more like a soccer team than a baseball team. Baseball is basically an accumulation of specialized, individual activities and achievement. The team that performs the most individual tasks well will likely win the game. In soccer, on the other hand, few of the tasks are individual. If you get the ball and your team mates have run the right formations, and structured the space around you, you'll have several options. Simon Critchley made this point well in the *New York Review of Books*, "Soccer is a collective game and everyone has to play the part which has been assigned to them, which means that they have to understand it... and make it effective."[3]

---

3   Brooks, David. "Baseball or Soccer." *New York Times*. N.p. n.d. Wed. 10 July, 2014.

Successful organizations are defined by the willingness and ability of almost everyone to

OWN their thoughts & emotions

OWN their reactions to people/situations

OWN their behaviors

OWN their words

OWN their attitude or mindset

OWN their personal & professional growth

OWN their mistakes/problems/solutions

OWN their success

Ownership isn't a passive experience, it's an active intentional one! Owners participate instead of spectate. Each of us can "take ownership" no matter what our position is in the organization. And not only on our "good days," but moment by moment each day, regardless of the circumstances, the people involved, our mood or the weather.

We must never forget that we are an amazingly talented collection of *adults* at work. Look around you and remind yourself how true this statement really is. As adults we are also deciders—we get to choose who to show up as and how to show up in every single interaction.

Doria, the evening front desk manager at the Fairfield Inn (at which I recently stayed) definitely displays an owner's mentality. She made it a point to tell me that if I needed anything, she was there to make it happen. She asked if I had had dinner; when I told her that I hadn't but I really didn't want to go back out in the deep freeze of East Coast winter, she quickly reviewed the delivery options with me. When I couldn't get my choice of restaurant to deliver a meal that evening, I called Doria. First, she called the restaurant to discuss the situation with the manager and express her disappointment. Then, she arranged for the Fairfield Inn van driver, Louis, to pick up my meal. He had an owner's mindset too. He delivered the meal to my room and wouldn't accept a gratuity! I've been back to that property twice since that experience—I returned because of Doria and Louis!

About seven years ago, I decided that question of owner versus renter was an urgent one that needed to be asked. Frequently. And with the intention of getting some honest answers. I decided to use my own version of a familiar and effective approach to get some answers. You've seen this approach on television and on YouTube—the man/woman on the street interview!

Here's how the Leta Beam version works: Whenever I visit an organization for the first time, I arrive early and mingle. Instead of being "on the street" I find one or two central spots; the cafeteria is a good option. Break rooms, fitness centers, and reception areas are also good choices. And I strike up brief informal conversations. Most people are friendly and willing to share their opinion with someone who actually listens. I tell them the truth about who I am: a leadership coach, a first-time visitor and a person genuinely interested in getting to know the organization. Then I pop the question! I ask every person, "Who's in charge of the success of this place?"

Before I tell you what I've learned so far, let me ask you: how would people in YOUR organization answer that question? How would you truthfully answer it?

_____

_____

_____

_____

Since I first began my woman/man on the street interviews there has been a sea change in the responses that I receive. Initially when I asked the question, "Who's in charge of the success of this place?" the unanimous response was someone other than me (the person responding). Some said the leaders, the bosses, the CEO or Executive Director. Others were even more vague—the higher ups or "them." One woman simply pointed skyward when I asked her the question! I couldn't resist saying, "Who, God?" No, that wasn't her meaning. Her gesture was intended to let me know that people on the executive floor were in charge.

At the time, I used any response to challenge our "same-old same-old" thinking on the issue of ownership and accountability. Hopefully I warmed the soil for a shift in perspective.

Now, fast forward seven years. The great news is that the responses have really changed! In the past year or so, about 40 percent of the people I ask say, "We are." That's a major breakthrough. I'm still waiting for the first person to look me in the eye and say, "I am personally responsible for this organization's success. I'm an owner!" I know it's coming soon!

So, what's it going to take to keep moving the needle? To increase that 40 percent to 60 percent? Even 70 percent and beyond? That powerful coaching question will carry on with us into the next chapter.

3

The Challenge: Changing Today's Renter Mentality

"I always wondered why somebody didn't do something about that. Then I realized that I was somebody."

Lily Tomlin, Comedian

Travis was definitely a "renter." He was a customer representative at a bank. By all appearances he was going through the motions at work. Low energy. Minimal interaction with me. Excused problems by blaming someone else for them. And finally told me that he was "putting in time" in this position until he found something better.

Why would Travis ever think that it is okay for him to just "put in time," until he "found something better?" And did he ever stop to think that perhaps nothing "better" would ever show up because of how he acted at his current job?

I closed the previous chapter with this question: "What's it going to take for more and more people to see themselves as personally responsible for the overall success of the organizations in which they work?"

If we're going to be more successful in embedding personal accountability in our workplaces, then we must first fully understand the business context that has shaped today's urgent need for new levels of ownership and the game changing foundation on which accountability-rich cultures are

17

developed. In other words, in order to build a culture of owners, we have to first find out what's in the way.

The Command and Control Model

How did so many of us end up as renters? It feels as though there should be a really complex answer to this powerful coaching question. But the truth is that I think it's actually pretty simple. I've come to believe that the traditional authoritarian, top-down organizational and leadership model cultivated and perpetuated a renter's mentality among a large segment of the work force!

Fortunately, I also believe that, today, this old school, traditional way of being together at work is on life support!

This "old way," commonly known as the command and control model, was built on the premise that "workers" were generally lazy, untrustworthy and stupid and needed to be watched and forced to do their work. In this model, a few people at the top of a steep organizational pyramid are "the leaders" and they make all of the important decisions. They tell everyone else what to do and how to do it. Everyone else pretty much carries out the directives and goes through the motions to get the work done.

The poster boy for this model was Frederick Taylor. During the Industrial Revolution his *Principles of Scientific Management* outlined a system to transfer all control from workers to management. He favored enforced standards and enforced cooperation. In his view, workers were incapable of understanding what they were doing, even the very simple tasks. So "enforcement" of work was the duty of management alone. One of his primary goals was to increase the distinction between mental (management) and manual (workers) labor. The worker had no responsibility for the overall outcome of the product; there was little to no pride in the work produced. The workers were simply "renters" doing their time, earning very little, and counting the days to retirement.

Even though the command and control model was originally applied to the emerging factory environments during the Industrial Revolution, over time, it became the dominant organizational and leadership model across most industries and disciplines. One of the reasons that I know this is that I grew up as a leader during the late 1980s and 1990s in a very large, bureaucratic organization and this command and control approach was alive and well there.

The Evolution of Corporate Culture

In *Take the Lead* I gave an example of how a culture can change from this "command and control" model to one that is more forward-looking. Ford Motor Company, a US owned automobile manufacturer, has broad name recognition in both the United States and internationally. Many people also would recognize its founder, Henry Ford, and identify him as an innovative industrialist who developed and manufactured the first automobile that middle class Americans could actually afford. Ford Motor Company was incorporated in 1903 and the Model T was introduced in 1908. Ford was a fan of Frederick Taylor. There is a quote, attributed to Henry Ford (although some experts doubt that Ford actually said these words) that captures his thinking vividly:

> *"Why is it that every time I ask for a pair of hands, they come with a brain attached?"*[4]

Regardless of whether he actually said it or not, it is a classic example of that early factory mentality in which workers were seen more as "human doings" rather than human beings; cogs in a very large machine.

Fast forward almost one hundred years. Bill Ford, the great grandson of Henry Ford, answered the call to lead the company into the twenty-first century. He knew that he had to make a different choice. Addressing thousands of Ford employees two years before the Great Recession of 2007 – 2009, he is reportedly quoted as saying:

> *"We can't keep playing the same old game the same old way and expect to have a sustainable future."*

---

4   Henry Ford. En.thinkexist.com

What a difference a century makes! Whether it's Ford, your local bank or a large regional health system, we are all navigating some powerful currents of change, the magnitude of which we haven't experienced in four decades.

As a direct result of this forceful change cycle, some of the **core elements of business are shifting dramatically**. Two in particular are relevant to our discussion: Organizational Structure and the very Nature of Leadership. The "same-old" organizational structure and leadership approach is the top down, authoritarian "command and control" model.

In *Take The Lead*, I highlight the fact that most thought leaders now consider this approach to leadership and relationships to be outdated and increasingly ineffective. It's still around in some organizations, but it's less and less effective and overwhelmingly rejected by the new generation of workers.

It is important to recognize its limitations. It's not going to carry us boldly into the future. It would be a terrible waste of time and talent for any of us to try to get better and better at this approach that just gets wrong-er and wrong-er. In fact, that approach is nothing more than a trap—you can never get better at something that doesn't work!

I have often said to those I work with, this isn't your father's—or mother's—workplace! Our work is increasingly complex, we're expected to move at a blistering pace, we are leaner, even resource strapped, and uncertainty and ambiguity are commonplace.

We can either choose to resist it, which is akin to throwing your hands up in front of a tsunami, or embrace it and give it shape. That means that we must "break with" old habits of thought and behavior and "break through" to new models and approaches; to view our relationships, our work and even ourselves through a prism of creativity and innovation.

So while the old model "isn't quite dead yet," a new brand of leadership is rapidly replacing it; one punctuated by an expectation that **leadership is a universal responsibility that everyone shares.** This is the "new normal," for which we're striving. And form is following function. To accommodate this more connected, collective leadership model, increasingly, organizational structures are flatter and more collaborative with broader opportunities for influence. Silo busting (meaning you're busting out of this "top down" control model) isn't an exception, it's the rule!

So Why the Fuss?

That's what you might be thinking right about now. If the old way of leading is on life support, then why not just let it fade on its own? Because it is too deeply ingrained in too many organizational cultures, and left to its own devices, it probably would never fully fade away. Command and control is the accepted way of being together and getting our work done and is part of our work DNA—it's embedded at a cellular level for many of us at work. As such, it is now rote thinking. It is the source of our habits because it's been drummed into our heads so often by so many, it now feels as though it's the way it has to be.

I can't stress this point enough. We have to fuss; we have to make ourselves move forward because we're pushing against belief that "it's a business truth and a truth for all times."

Think about it. We've gotten so used to being bossed around—told what to do and when to do it—and we're so used to feeling disappointed, frustrated, powerless and even cynical, that we're numb to it all. Even though we don't like it, it feels familiar and safe. Dysfunctional comfort at your service! So, even though many of us are waking up to the urgent need to change and behave differently, we're not quite sure how to pull it off.

My experience at a New York restaurant epitomizes this pattern. Mark, a member of the wait staff was pleasant and seemed competent. The trouble began when I wanted to substitute a small salad for the French fries that came with my meal (now aren't I a healthy eater!). He informed me about the "no substitution" policy. He then went on to explain that he thought it was a stupid rule instituted by the corporate office and if it were up to him, customers could make healthy substitutions. He was just doing what he was told. He said that he had "given up" offering feedback on the subject because no one cares what he thinks. Finally, he encouraged me to register a formal complaint with the manager in the hopes that burying the company in negative feedback would get them to change.

Changing organizational cultures from "renter" to "owner," is going to take a lot more than a new slogan or the latest "program." It's the same call to action that Bill Ford challenged his company with in 2005: to shake up our "same-old same-old" thoughts and behaviors. We need to be free to find the courage to approach our relationships at work differently so that we can co-create a markedly different and intentionally brighter future together.

Margaret Wheatley, author of *Leadership and the New Science*, has said that we "need nothing short of a revolution." I've become convinced that she's right. We can't afford to wait any longer for things to evolve on their own. There's too much at stake and our point of power is NOW. I don't think we can continue to work and be successful without being engaged, without being treated as smart, well-intended adults and without a much broader distribution of power, authority and leadership…in other words, without a prevailing mentality of ownership.

Accountability's Enduring Foundation

In *Take the Lead*, I discussed two highly influential transformative forces that need to be discussed before we go any further because together, they represent the sparks that ignite our willingness and desire to change who we are and what we do at work. I have excerpted parts of that book here so you can understand what must be done first to ultimately create a culture of accountable leaders who are owning not just their work but are taking on the responsibility for the entire organization. For a full understanding of these two points, I invite you to read *Take the Lead*.

Here they are:

1. The Shift From Positional to Relationship Leadership.

Today, relationship trumps position. According to the rules of the command and control model, leadership was defined by one's title, position, salary level and whether or not you had a corner office. This positional brand of leadership rigidly separated leaders from followers. In the emerging relational leadership model, I don't do your bidding simply because of your position; rather, we value one another's contribution, come from a place of mutual respect, aim ourselves in the same direction and practice both leadership and followership to achieve our co-created goals. We behave as though everyone counts and every seat in the organization is a power seat.

I call this "leading from your seat," and guess what, **everyone leads from his/her seat!** What exactly does that mean? It means that each person makes a personal commitment to show up as the best version themselves each day at work. And throughout the day, we *own the moment*, rarely, if ever, settling for mediocrity. Or being good enough.

> *Think about this: For those of us who have kids, we've had the experience of putting them on the school bus or dropping them at school and sending them off with a thought for the day; something like, "Have a great day!" "Try your very best!" "Do well on that math test!"*
>
> *Was there ever a time when you said, "Be mediocre today!" "Don't work too hard!" "Don't push yourself to get a good grade on that math test." Or, "don't be too great today, you don't want to outshine your classmates."*
>
> *If you're laughing because the very idea of saying those things is pretty ridiculous, I agree. Then why would we settle for anything less that owning each moment at work? What message are we routinely sending ourselves!*

This point is the lynchpin to the development of an accountability-rich organization, so it bears repeating: As more and more of us lead from our seats and accept the universal responsibility of leadership, an owner's mentality is the natural byproduct! The redefinition of leadership acts as the catalyst for creating a culture of owners.

What does it look like and feel like when you choose to lead from your seat at work? This is what I've seen happen:

- ✪ You know your job inside and out.
- ✪ Every day, you routinely ask yourself, "Am I doing what needs to be done?"
- ✪ Every day you look for ways to do it differently and better. You prepare suggestions and ideas for how to make things better and you share them with others to get feedback.
- ✪ Throughout the day, you take stock of how things are going and what you can do to be more useful and effective.
- ✪ You know what others do and how what you do blends with their "stuff" for the good of the organization.

✪ You see yourself as an owner of the organization. It does not fall to someone else to make this a great place to work and really, really successful. It's *your* job.

✪ You do your work well, creatively, with grit and gusto. You bring your best self to work. No excuses.

✪ You acknowledge that you may only have part of the picture and others may have ideas that are both different from and better than yours.

✪ You avoid constant comparisons of the type and amount of your contribution versus another team member. You are only in charge of you and you choose to model leadership behavior.

✪ You actively help others to be their best. And you give them permission to help you by opening yourself to constructive feedback from those around you.

✪ You make it a habit to applaud and support others' efforts to make positive changes and improvements in their work.

✪ You listen with a cooperative ear to proposed organizational changes that will require you to change, too. You listen for opportunities to be even better at your duties.

✪ You are regularly tuned in to your self-talk and your emotions, so that you continually choose those constructive thoughts and feelings that will reinforce new habits and move you and your organization forward.

This point hit home for me during a recent stay at a Marriott property in San Diego, California USA. It was very early morning (4:45AM!) and my husband, Jim and I were heading out the door and to the airport for our return flight. A member of the bell team, Reggie, approached us immediately and offered apologies for not having a taxi waiting for us (no, we did not arrange for a taxi the night before). He explained that he always liked to have at least two cabs waiting and both had just left with fares. He informed us that a cab was five minutes away. He left and returned with two bottles of water and said, "Here's some water for you folks while you wait. I'm really sorry about this delay. This is my hotel and I know that if you don't have an extraordinary time here, you may not come back. And I want you back!" Our taxi pulled up, he shook our hands, we gave him a generous tip and off we went. Once in the cab, my husband looked at me and said, "Now that guy gets it!" And I agreed. Imagine being WOW'd at 4:45AM!! Oh, by the way, we're going back to that property in a few months.

Setting a new expectation that leadership is a universal responsibility that each person shares is the best preparatory step to activating a sense of personal accountability across your organization. It "warms the soil," allowing accountability to move in and become a deeply rooted cultural value and norm.

2. Reaching for Full-Throttle Engagement

No review of the game changing foundation on which accountability is built would be complete without a hardy discussion of the second influential force, **full throttle engagement**. When you "lead from your seat," and own your work you become predisposed to higher levels of engagement. Not just engagement…..full-throttle engagement!

The word "engagement" gets tossed around a lot in many organizations and yet, when I ask, people struggle to tell me what it means to them. So, let's make sure that we have a shared understanding of its definition. My research and my experiences working with hundreds of diverse organizations has led me to a realization that

> *Workplace engagement is, at its core, an emotional attachment that someone feels for the work that they do; the people with whom they do it; and the organization of which they are a part that profoundly influences the person's willingness to learn, grow, and perform at higher levels.*
>
> *Engaged team members are fully involved and enthusiastic about their work; this leads them to act, more often than not, in ways that mutually serve both their own and the organization's interests.*

The punchy descriptor, *full-throttle*, acts as a booster rocket, delivering a heightened level of intensity and commitment that comes close to missionary zeal. Instead of just saying the words, "We're all in this together," we actually live those words day in and day out.

When I visit an organization for the first time, I look for the following behaviors, attitudes and mindsets. The more of them that I experience, the further along the organization is on its journey to high levels of engagement.

- ✪ Almost everyone leads from their seats and act as owners.
- ✪ Almost everyone adopts a framework of possibility & positivism
- ✪ Almost every person owns the success of the **entire organization**
- ✪ Almost everyone is personally aligned with the organization's vision, mission, values
- ✪ Almost everyone fosters high quality relationships
- ✪ Almost everyone commits to learning & un-learning
- ✪ Almost everyone has demonstrates a bias to effective communication
- ✪ There is a habit of celebrating together (often)

Here are a few examples of statements that focus on a person's level of engagement:

- ★ This organization inspires me to do my very best.
- ★ I am willing to put in a great deal of effort in order to contribute to my organization's success.
- ★ I look forward to coming to work most days.
- ★ I have strong relationships with my team mates.
- ★ I would recommend this organization to anyone as a great place to work.
- ★ I am regularly recognized for my contributions.
- ★ I am likely to be working for this organization three years from now.

How about you? The more of these that are characteristic of your current feeling about work, the more engaged you tend to be.[5]

---

5 The following research sites were influential in developing the definition of engagement: "Glossary." Www.Hrzone.com. N.p., n.d. Web; Www.Businessdictionary.com. N.p., n.d. Web; Www.library.ucsb.edu. N.p., n.d. Web.

Is The Work Worth It?

How do we know that this sense of ownership can deliver a more satisfying, rewarding and successful experience at work? If we're to commit to transforming our way of life at work (and that is *exactly* what we're talking about here) then we need some pretty compelling evidence that it's all worth it. Here's what did it for me and why I'm all in when it comes to shifting from a culture of renters to a culture full of owners:

1. The Success of Employee Owned Organizations

    The jury is back and the verdict is IN! There is a substantial (and growing) body of research that supports the idea that employee ownership leads to high performance levels in both the UK as well as in the United States. The work of Joseph Blasi from Rutgers and Richard Freeman from Harvard is particularly impressive because of the quality of its principle researchers and the source of the data, The Great Place to Work Institute (I am a huge fan!). In a review of their book, *The Citizen's Share*, Christopher Matthews artfully and succinctly summarizes the key findings. He says, "…the authors' research shows that on average, firms which give employees an ownership stake are more productive, more innovative and more desirable workplaces for employees. Employee ownership pays off…"[6]

2. Engagement Equals Success

    Those of you who have read *Take the Lead*, already know the profound impact that high levels of employee engagement have on business success. According to Wagner and Harter, who work for the Gallup polling service, workgroups whose engagement levels put them in the bottom quartile of the Gallup database average 62 percent more accidents. On the other hand, engaged employees average 27 percent less absenteeism. Teams in the top engaged quartiles are three times more likely to succeed as those in the bottom quartile, averaging 18 percent higher productivity

---

6   Joseph R. Blasi, Richard B. Freeman, and Douglas L. Kruse. *The Citizen's Share: Putting Ownership Back into Democracy.* New Haven, Connecticut: Yale University Press, 2013. Print.

and 12 percent higher profitability.[7]

★ When we act as owners, we are naturally more emotionally attached to our work, our colleagues and our organizations.

★ We allow that emotional attachment to lift our individual and collective performance to new levels.

★ A virtuous cycle is born.

That's what engagement is all about. Engagement and ownership are linked in an exchange of great energy.

3. Practical Wisdom

Is it just me or is this a duh, forehead-smacking moment? I'm a huge fan of the kind of hard core, quantitative proof that's discussed in points 1 & 2 above. But I think most of us already knew that a strong sense of ownership would deliver great results. Do your own gut check. My intuitive intelligence, my gut, tells me that if you "own it"—your work, your decisions, your behaviors, your choices, your relationships—you're going to care more, do more than expected, show up as the best version of yourself more often and be more successful! And I trust my gut! What is yours telling you right now?

So let's connect the dots. If employee-owned organizations perform better than others on many key metrics, and if engaged employees enjoy higher performance levels and more happiness at work than their non-engaged counterparts, then, it stands to reason, that fostering more tangible opportunities to experience ownership and accepting and exploiting those opportunities day in and day out will lead us to more success. When we genuinely connect our heads, our hearts and our guts and tap into our own practical wisdom, it simply makes sense.

Tearing Down the Wall

If we're serious about creating an accountability-rich culture in which the overwhelming majority of workers are engaged, leading from their seat, and viewing their workplace through the leadership lens of OWNERSHIP, then we have to go beyond merely acknowledging that the renter's mentality

---

7   Wagner, Rodd, and James K. Harter. *The Elements of Great Management*. New York: Gallup Press, 2006. Print.

is still entrenched in many organizations today. We must recognize the role that we have played in keeping it alive through our action or inaction.

Many a wise person has said that the thing that gets in your way most often is *you*. It's sometimes a hard truth to face, but I have found it to be highly accurate. Sure we can blame our culture, our bosses, the CEO or the Board of Directors, even our co-workers for the non-optimal working conditions in which we find ourselves. However—

never lose sight of the fact that individually and collectively we are a powerful force with which to be reckoned. Our culture will change one conversation at a time; one relationship at a time; and one choice at a time.

When we recognize and acknowledge the role we have played in keeping the "same-old same-old" culture at work, even if it is a small role, then we are primed to make a different choice.

Here's a mind-storming exercise that can help us to comprehensively consider that powerful idea and help you find a way to constructively change your thinking about your workplace. Take a look at this picture of a stone wall.

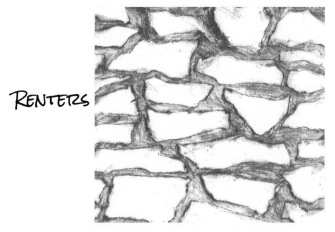

RENTERS   OWNERS

Think of each stone as something that gets in the way of being, working, and achieving greatness as a culture of owners. The stones together create a wall. On the far side of the wall is a workplace culture of owners who individually and collectively choose accountability. On the near side is a workplace culture dominated more often than not by a renter's mentality, where somebody (anybody but me) else is accountable for our success.

✪ Your first assignment is to come clean and tell yourself the unvarnished truth about which side of the wall your team/organization most often operates. For those of us who have been living fully on the far side of this wall, I say do the happy dance, it's worth celebrating your courageous new habits. For some of us, we may have scaled this wall from time to time and ended up on the far side; but we still spend most of our work time on the near side. And for many of us, we're pretty much stuck on the near side. Again, there's no right or wrong answer here. It's simply a matter of acknowledging where you are today.

On which side of the wall do you live?

_____

✪ Your second assignment is a challenge to drill down in your thinking and wade into the specifics.

★ If your culture is dominated by a renter's mentality today, I want you to write one thing on each stone in the wall (on the facing page) that is keeping you and your colleagues from becoming that culture of owners. Feel free to invite other members of your team to contribute suggestions. For example, I included a very traditional leadership approach on one of my stones. Another was bosses who act like parents. Now it's your turn. The intention here is to provoke some thinking. No looking ahead to check out my answers!

★ If your culture has shifted to an owner's mentality, then I ask that you take a look in the rearview mirror and identify the hurdles that had to be overcome during your transformation, brick by brick. It's a helpful and often overlooked step to tell ourselves how things got "right" so that we can use that awareness the next time we face a challenge. You also might be surprised to find that there are some stubborn obstacles that remain in your way!

Notes:

_____

_____

_____

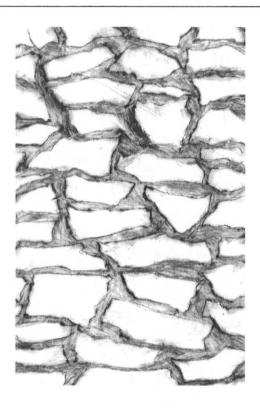

So what? What have we learned? We know more clearly what's been blocking our progress; we know what's been stonewalling us!

The only way you can fix anything is first figuring out what's not working. These stones represent what is getting in your way. But don't think of them as insurmountable. That will stop you from ever moving forward and achieving greatness as an owner. Rather, consider this quote from Randy Pausch's famous _The Last Lecture_:

"*The brick walls are there for a reason. The brick walls are not there to keep us out. The brick walls are there to give us a chance to show how badly we want something. The brick walls are there to stop people who don't want it badly enough.*" [8]

Here's how I chose to complete this learning exercise:

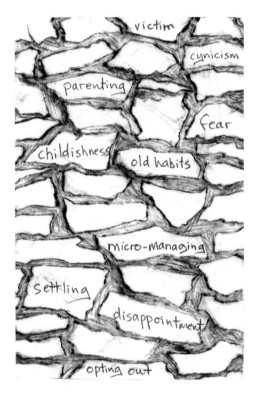

Rather than stopping you, I hope the stone wall you have created here in this exercise stokes your sparks of possibility and propels you forward.

---

8   Randy Pausch. *The Last Lecture*. New York: Hyperion Books, 2008. Print.

So let's circle back to our powerful coaching question: "What's it going to take for more and more people to see themselves as personally responsible for the overall success of the organizations in which they work?"

Answer: de-constructing the wall, of course. If these are the things that are in our way, then let's work on one stone at a time and remove it from the wall. Then another. You may be pleasantly surprised at how fast that wall can come down with everyone chipping away at it.

Much of the remainder of this Everyday Leadership book is your invitation to reach for the leadership version of a pick and shovel to take that wall down. I want you to take your wall down stone by stone until there's nothing standing in your way from enjoying the success that "accountability on steroids" can shower on an organization.

PART ONE

Setting the Stage

HIGHLIGHTS

The Endgame: A Culture of Owners, Not Renters

- ✪ Co-creating a bright future together in our organization hinges on fostering and sustaining a culture full of individuals with an owner's mentality rather than a renter's.

- ✪ Ownership isn't a passive experience. It's an active, intentional one.

- ✪ Cliff Hakim's latest edition of his ground breaking book, *We Are All Self-Employed*, is a wise selection as a supplemental reference.

- ✪ Take the leadership dare: Find an unbiased way to ask the question, "Who's in charge of the success of this place?" at your workplace. Discuss the results with your colleagues.

_____

_____

_____

_____

The Challenge: Changing Today's Renter Mentality

- ✪ The renter's mentality is still alive in some organizations.

- ✪ Our choice of action or inaction has allowed this way of thinking and behaving to continue.

- ✪ The traditional authoritarian, top down organizational and leadership model cultivated and continues to perpetuate the renter's mindset.

✪ The current leadership model has shifted from that traditional "positional" brand of leadership to a relationship based one. To create an environment that fosters and fuels accountability, everyone must share the responsibility and show up, leading from their seats, as the best version of themselves. Collective and connected leadership is the enduring foundation for a culture that places high value on personal accountability.

✪ There is compelling evidence that fostering more tangible opportunities to experience ownership will lead us to more success.

✪ _____

_____

_____

_____

PART
TWO

ACCOUNTABILITY:
WHAT IT'S ALL ABOUT

4

Finding Your Way to Accountability

I've been talking about "accountability" this and "owning" that. But what does accountability mean?

When I talk to groups and individuals about accountability, it's always interesting to watch their response. To me accountability is the gritty stuff of our work life—owning the moment, one decision at a time, one choice at a time. It can lift you up to a new level of leadership maturity and personal gratification; and when these personal shifts become widespread, they can elevate an entire organization.

Part One explored why the current "same-old same-old" isn't working—and perhaps hasn't ever fully worked—in organizations. We talked about how leading from your seat and full-throttle engagement form a sustainable foundation on which to build a strong framework of personal accountability.

Once this foundation is in the place, the best next, and most important, step in creating an accountability-rich culture is to develop a shared understanding of exactly what "accountability" means. That is the sole purpose of Part Two. And here's a hint. By the time you read my definition of accountability, it shouldn't be some grand revelation. It should invoke more of an "of course, that's what it is," response." But also know that while the idea of accountability is at heart wonderfully simple, it isn't easy.

The Accountability Compass

A compass is a vital tool when negotiating both known and unknown territory. Like accountability, it is a wonderfully simple tool that isn't always easy to use. But once you've mastered it, it can point you in the right direction, keeps you on the right track, and helps you find your way if you ever get lost.

Let me share a visual with you that, I think, powerfully portrays the interrelatedness of the foundational elements vetted in Part One and the fearless practice of personal accountability. I call it the Accountability Compass. It artfully captures the flow among the elements: lead from your seat, act as an owner, be fully engaged, be fearlessly accountable—one being dependent upon the rest and none being more important than the other. Here's what it looks like:

While I have purposefully not given you the definition of accountability—yet—it's not hard to deduce what this means from what we already know: The robust relationships between all team members in an organization, no matter what their rank, are formed as more people choose to lead from their seat. This creates the emotional attachment of engagement through which people act more like an owner than a renter. From this new vantage point, one chooses personal accountability more and more often. I call this a "virtuous cycle," for it repeats itself over and over again as individuals in the organization grow stronger and a healthier, more effective and more satisfying workplace emerges.

This compass is key because it will guide us throughout the rest of our discussion on accountability and illuminate the inspired actions you must undertake to achieve it intrinsically in your organization. We have touched on the first three in Part One, but again, I invite you to read *Take the Lead* in its entirety to see the heights to which "leading from your seat," acting as an owner and being fully engaged can take a willing, determined organization. Personal accountability is fed by these three things and in turn refuels these three things.

Now it is time to take the "deep dive," as I often say, into this wonderful world of accountability. But because accountability is not, unfortunately, necessarily a given in many organizational cultures, I think that the best way to advance a definition of accountability is to, first, strip away outdated, maladaptive ideas about it. I first want to show you what it isn't!

Beyond the Buzzwords

Accountability is a word that gets thrown around…a lot. We already talk a lot about accountability at work. Walk down any hallway, pass any office, eavesdrop on a meeting or read through your emails, and you'll find the word mentioned frequently. And, in my experience, use of the word *accountability* is often accompanied by a sense of frustration, blame, cynicism or disappointment. But I quickly realized that all that talk is just that—superficial talk!

But *accountability* is not just about using a buzz word, is it? That's not going to help us co-create a culture of people being accountable. It's about having effective, relevant, adult conversations that create a shared understanding of what accountability means to us in our organization—what it looks like and feels like in everyday interactions.

An accountability-rich culture is about asking questions and allowing the person to come to their own conclusion. To tell someone what to do or "how to be accountable," would be to fall right back into the "same-old same-old" stream that I have been swimming against for the past twenty years.

Here are some powerful coaching questions to consider as you think about accountability:

- ✪ **Does your organization have a clear definition of workplace accountability that has been shared with every team member?**
- ✪ **Have you clearly identified the set of behaviors and the mindset that are consistent with that definition?**
- ✪ **Have you clearly identified attitudes and behaviors that are inconsistent with your definition?**

In my experience, accountability is that one critical piece to the organizational puzzle of sustainable success. Yet few of us really understand what it really means. And even fewer are creating the structure that will allow it to take root and flourish.

It seems to me that we've adopted the "cross your fingers" approach to culturally embedding accountability as a core value. We cross our fingers and hope that if we use the word accountability often enough, then somehow we'll all become accountable. It often sounds something like...

- ✪ *"We all need to be accountable."*
- ✪ *"I'm going to hold you accountable."*
- ✪ *"Who's supposed to be accountable for this?"*
- ✪ *"You have to do a better job of holding her accountable!"*
- ✪ *"No one's being accountable."*
- ✪ *"We've got to hold each other accountable."*
- ✪ *"Why am I the only one following through on our commitments?"*
- ✪ *"This is good enough."*
- ✪ *"That's not my job."*

When the phone rings in the Vantage office, there's a strong likelihood that the person on the other end of the line will be looking for help in "holding other people accountable."

The conversation goes something like this: "We need you to come and teach us how to hold _____ (Fill in the blank with the name of a department or a team, some group of people, or the entire organization) accountable!"

Here's my standard, and somewhat provocative response, "I'm going to save you a lot of money because my services aren't inexpensive. My coaching truth is that you can't really hold others accountable!" After a few moments of stunned silence, the person recovers and a useful discussion of the issue usually follows.

"A strange thing, words. Once they're said,
it's hard to imagine they're untrue."

Sharon Biggs Waller

Unfortunately, I know what most people mean when they use the popular phrase, "hold others accountable." It's code for, "There are people in our organization who aren't doing what they're supposed to do. And we really need them to do what they're supposed to do. Teach us some new techniques to get them to do the right thing regularly. What we're doing today hasn't worked very well." So, if everyone knows the code, then what's the big deal?

Words have real power and we must choose them intentionally and wisely if we are to have a shot at being honest with ourselves and getting our real message across to others. Words create filters through which we view our world. They can have a dramatic impact on what we know, how we interact with people and the decisions we make. And right now, it's my strong sense that many of us are using the phrase "hold others account-able," without really thinking through the unintended assumptions and consequences with which it may be associated.

Right about now, some of you might be asking yourself if this is about "wordsmithing." I've thought about that question at length and my answer is a definite No. This is not a "you say 'tomayto,' I say 'tomaato'" situation. It runs much deeper than that.

From my vantage point, there is a subtle but real danger inherent in the phrase, "hold others accountable." Part One has offered a pretty credible argument that, if we're to have a bright, successful future, then we need to show up as adults in the workplace—as deciders and choosers. In other words, as owners! It is both logical and intuitive to conclude that we adults must *choose* to **be** accountable. That means that it's intrinsic, it comes from within, not without. You can hold yourself accountable but you can't make someone else "accountable." They will choose to be accountable or not.

The other equally serious drawback that I see in perpetuating the phrase "hold others accountable," is that it reinforces the parent/child dynamic, a stale leftover from the Industrial Age that is still hanging on in some organizations. I think that children in their early formative years do not have the full capacity to be accountable. That's why we create family rules, carefully supervise them, even look over their shoulders, and threaten them with punishment. But is that the best model from which to build an effective organizational culture? Seriously?

Let's call it like it is. If you're going to continue to apply external pressure in an attempt to force someone else to be accountable, then what you're going to get is nothing more than compliance at best or malicious obedience at worst. When it's compliance, the person either wants to earn a perceived reward (the proverbial "carrot") or avoid the punishment (the "stick"). The trouble with compliance is that the pressure always has to be there. Malicious obedience is even more troublesome. A person gives the appearance of complying by doing the absolute minimum to avoid the stick. Along the way, they drag their feet, resist, and occasionally sabotage the effort while recruiting others to their "cause." Sound familiar?

"Words have power… If you have the right words, there's nothing on earth you can't do."

Lori Handeland, Crave The Moon

Let's come off auto pilot, think purposefully about the message we truly want to send here and stop using the phrase "hold others accountable" out of habit.

In light of all we discussed, what if we used the following phrases when thinking and acting on accountability?

✪ I'm choosing to be accountable (in this situation). I encourage you to do the same.

✪ Each of us and all of us must make the adult choice to be accountable if our organization is to thrive.

✪ I (and/or our organization) expect that each of us practices personal accountability day in and day out. Here's how we define accountability here.

✪ How can I help you to *hold yourself accountable* to our standards?

The Trap

The last question above is a key orientation point in this path towards accountability. It has to do with your actions and those of others.

Have you ever been in a situation where you knew someone's actions were wrong but you did nothing because you were afraid—for your job, your reputation, even your perceived piece of mind? Have you ever caught yourself thinking, "I don't want to get involved," because you knew it would be a difficult, uncomfortable event, to face the adversity you knew was being created?

Accountability has to do with how we act. As you read the following story, ask yourself, "how would I have acted in this situation?"

Hannah was the new leader of an administrative support team of approx-imately ninety members, working across three shifts. She followed a popular team leader, who left to take a position that had a less demanding schedule so that she could attend to some pressing personal matters. Ten people left the department shortly thereafter. Those who remained were left to cover vacancies across all shifts. They were hurt, frustrated and overwhelmed; some felt as though the exiting leader had given up on them; abandoned them.

Hannah arrived with lots of energy to share and began to see ways in which things could be better and different for the team and their clients. She was excited, confident that she could make a difference and eager to begin. She attempted to get the staff involved in committees to brainstorm and find solutions to some tough and long-standing problems.

Some team members were intrigued by some of Hannah's ideas and willing to give them a try; others were lukewarm, choosing to take a wait and see approach. A few were openly critical of what Hannah had to offer. Two of the team's informal leaders, Jeri and Harper, went a step further and took every opportunity to be cynical, dismissive and disrespectful. They mis-directed their bitterness and disappointment at Hannah instead of welcoming her and giving her the benefit of the doubt. They worked behind the scenes, engaging in a "whispering campaign," trash talking Hannah behind her back and recruiting others to their "cause."

As a result, very little progress was made in Hannah's first three months on the job. Her enthusiasm waned and her self-confidence took a hit. She left for another position after five months. While it wasn't the sole reason, Jeri and Harper's middle school behaviors did weigh heavily on Hannah's decision. They missed the mark on accountability by a mile!

Recruiting another team leader became more difficult as word about the team dynamics spread internally and externally and its reputation became tarnished. Several other members left. The team remained adrift and work product suffered. Ultimately, the unit was disbanded and the work restructured. A lack of accountability played a significant role in the root cause of this failure. The consequences of Jeri and Harper's decision to act as they did were severe, not only for Hannah, but for the entire team and the organization as well.

Hannah did her best to take those first baby steps toward the creation of a culture of accountability, but her teammates classically resisted, and because few, if any, were holding themselves personally accountable, things spiraled down pretty quickly.

I remember how uncomfortable I felt when I first learned of this situation. I couldn't help thinking, "It didn't need to end this way. Those team members *knew* what was going on. Why didn't someone stand up for what was right?" That's a complicated question to answer, and leads us directly into the heart of accountability.

But before I go there, let me ask you this: if you were Hannah, what would you have done differently to have a different outcome? What if you were a member of her team?

5

Orienting Towards the Positive

A negative definition only works if it can create an opposite, positive flow. Hannah's story has vividly showcased what accountability isn't. It's not really a huge jump to orient that towards the positive.

Fortunately, there are plenty of examples of team members in an organization acting in ways as fully accountable adults. The first is directly opposite of the Hannah fiasco, and it's one of my favorites:

Sue Ann is a member of a project team in the food service industry. She is an asset to the team and gets along well with most. She is also introverted and tends to dislike attention and conflict, so many times, she flies below the radar. But when two senior members of the team began to mistreat and even bully a newer member from another department, she found her inner strength and directly confronted the behavior with the two individuals involved. Because she was not one to speak up frequently, her feedback surprised her colleagues and made them stop and think. She continued to single-handedly turn this situation around by also reaching out to the new team member and offering reassuring support. She took a risk to do the right thing. The behavior stopped and she has a new-found confidence.

Then there was Andrew.

It's difficult and humbling to admit your role in a mistake. But it's the right thing to do. And, that's exactly what happened to Andrew. He was working on a client file/system and accidentally deleted it without proper backup three days before the project's deadline. He admitted the situation to his boss; offered a plan to make it right; and was willing to work around the clock to make it happen. He also participated in re-negotiating the timeline and delivered the

work a day early. He was willing to accept the consequence of his mistake.
Much to his relief, he was not dismissed; his boss simply wanted to be sure
that he learned from the mistake and that it wouldn't happen again.

If we expect our colleagues to make dozens, even hundreds, of decisions each day about what to do and who to be using a framework of accountability as their guide, then it only stands to reason that we make darn sure that there is a universal understanding of exactly what that means. And that has everything to do with Andrew's willingness to accept the consequences of his mistakes (which is also a very good definition of what it means to be "grown up" if you think about it.)

So, having looked at both what it is and what it isn't, what does *accountability* mean to you? If your organization has a working definition that is helpful to you, then use it. If not, write down your personal take on accountability. There's one caveat: Define accountability without using the word "accountable" in it.

_____

_____

_____

_____

_____

_____

_____

Now it's my turn to share my coaching definition. To be candid, most dictionary definitions of accountability seem inadequate to me and leave me cold. So, based on my research, I crafted one that empowers and inspires everyday leadership and is straightforward enough so that everyone can understand it and use it "in the moment" to assess the quality of their decisions and choices. Here it is:

5 • Orienting Towards the Positive

Personal Workplace Accountability is doing the right thing consistently, day after day, in both tasks and relationships to live the Mission and Values of the organization and advance its Vision.[9]

Remember when I said in the introduction to Part Two that this should be somewhat anticlimactic? If the previous chapters have done the trick and gotten the message across effectively, you had a really good grasp of it already.

This definition of *accountability* is based on the simple yet profound belief that most people know what the right thing to do is most of the time. Yes, at times there are gray areas, but *most of the time, most of us* know. Whether we choose to act on that knowledge is at the heart of the matter. For example, almost all of us know that gossip is toxic in organizations. But do we accept personal responsibility for walking away when it starts, choosing not to engage in it with others and, even confronting the behavior and encouraging others to change the subject?

"A time may come when you have to make a choice between what is right and what is easy."

Professor Dumbledore to Harry Potter in *Harry Potter and the Goblet of Fire*

---

9   In 2010 I began working on what accountability really means—what a good, easy to comprehend, definition might be. I decided that, at its core, it was about doing the right thing consistently, regardless of circumstances, in order to meet the mission of the organization, live its values and fulfill the vision.

I read so many articles about accountability and many of them really missed the mark for me. But I found several that resonated with similar themes/definitions. They viewed accountability in the same way that I did. Two in particular emphasized that it was about doing the right thing. The articles/sites that are referenced here had almost identical definitions to the one that I drafted. I found that to be really cool and affirming; I was on the right track! I also found an element of Marcia Rachel's definition to be very important and I added it to enhance my own—to refine it. The phrase—in both task and relationship—was not in my original definition.

I'd like to fully acknowledge Ms. Rachel's influence on my current definition of accountability: Marcia Rachel. M., Ph.D. "Accountablity: A Concept Worth Revisiting." *AmericanNurse Today*.com. See also www.timewellscheduled.com.

That's why I've come to believe that personal accountability is an inside job! Doing the right thing comes from within; it's intrinsic. When doing the right thing comes from the outside, when it becomes extrinsic instead, then it becomes nothing more than compliance. I am convinced that relying primarily on compliance will prevent us from being great and having a bright future together.

Right about now, some of you might be thinking, "That's great, BUT… if accountability is intrinsic, isn't it a part of your hardwiring?" OR, "isn't accountability something that is embedded in your psyche from early experiences and reinforcement by adults important in our lives (parents, grandparents, teachers, religious leaders)?" If you didn't "get it" then, maybe you've missed out permanently.

My answers are yes, yes and no. Yes, it may be that a predisposition to hold oneself accountable is hardwired; and yes, it might seem more natural to us if we were exposed to it regularly as kids when we discussed it as a family or when we witnessed our parents and others role modeling the behavior.

But no, if this isn't the case for you, you haven't missed out on the opportunity to be an accountable adult today! It's my truth that each of us does have a unique genetic endowment and experiences in our formative years. And, while I can't claim expertise in genetics, my review of the research tells me that education and personal effort can trump your starting point. Even our genes require regular input as we grow and develop to work properly. Don't use your genes or your background as an excuse not to embrace personal accountability.

Adopting the Accountability Credo

My bottom line is that, to a large extent, *personal accountability can be learned and is a choice that adults can intentionally make.*

Because it is a choice, to be "fearlessly accountable" requires some work. It's not always easy to simply "do the right thing." But what if we had a guide to help us, especially when something happens that lies in that very "gray" area between right and wrong?

To that end, I have created an Accountability Credo. A *credo* is a statement of the beliefs or aims that guide someone's actions.[10] To have a workplace in which most/all people are accountable we must begin by recognizing and adopting the following beliefs:

Acccountability Credo

➤ *We are a group of* CAPABLE *adults.* ➤

➤ *Most people want to do* CREDIBLE *work.*
They want to be good,
even GREAT *at work.* ➤

➤ *We ultimately* CHOOSE *or decide*
how to 'BE' *at work.* ➤

➤ ACCOUNTABILITY *is an adult choice.* ➤

➤ *Our shared* RESPONSIBILITY *is to*
CO-CREATE *the environmental conditions*
that foster and REWARD *that choice*
so that it's EMBEDDED *in the very fiber,*
the DNA, *of the organization.* ➤

---

10   https://www.merriam-webster.com/dictionary/credo

Think of the Accountability Credo as the magnetic needle of the Accountability compass. It helps point the way towards right action. Like the definition of accountability, it is simple and straightforward, but it is not always easy to do because, for some, it pushes our buttons by fundamentally challenging our current ways of thinking, acting and believing.

Here is your challenge: allow the Accountability Credo to become your statement of belief that guides your everyday actions. See yourself and others as everyday heroes and think of accountability as your superpower! It may just be a power that can change your world.

Accountability Prerequisites

Now that we know what we're aiming for, where and how do we start? Sometimes, it's tough to even know where to begin the work of getting to a different and better place. Given the pace at which we work and the sheer volume of stuff that needs to get done, we could be tempted to look for a quick fix. I don't think one exists that will get you the results that you want and need.

In order to set ourselves up for success, we need to roll up our sleeves and start at the very beginning. Back to basics. We need to develop a new brand of everyday conversation to deliver this simple but powerful message. This is "small picture" action—the words, behaviors, beliefs, attitudes and assumptions (and more) that we choose regularly.

But before we dive into that "small picture" stuff (what's coming in Part Three), we need to do all that we can as leaders from our seats to be sure that the "big picture" portrays the same message and provides a sturdy framework to move forward.

So to close Part Two, I want to think big picture. Here are some bright ideas to continue to "warm the soil" for accountability to take root and grow into a way of life that defines your culture:

- ✪ Create universal (yes, that means absolutely everyone!) knowledge and understanding of the vision, mission, values, strategies and goals of the organization AND help everyone to make the connection between them and the choices they make each day at work. People want to believe that what they do has meaning; that they are contributing to a larger good. The best way to demonstrate the value of someone's work is to show them how it fits into the "bigger picture." No one needs to be able to recite the vision or mission. In fact, rote memory won't get the real job done. Instead, let's have conversations about the meaning behind these elements. Let's talk about them in our own words – What does this mean to you? Help each person to "get the picture." This is what owners do! Owners are attached to the vision, mission and values with both their hearts and their heads. And the realization that the small tasks that I perform each day actually do relate to these big, hairy, audacious goals – well, it can be a goose bump moment. It fuels a sense of pride, alignment and commitment. Can you feel the energy that would be released in these new (or renewed) conversations? Woo Hoo!

✪ Define accountability in simple, straightforward terms that a 12 year old would understand! I made sure that my definition qualifies! Feel free to use it in its entirety or make it your own by tweaking it. Review and refresh regularly. Just because we use the term in every other sentence doesn't mean that there is a shared definition of accountability in the organization. Let's make it so by including it in every on-boarding class; every learning program; staff meetings, on our intra-net, in our publications – think saturation. Let's use real examples, situations, and case studies to drive our point home.

✪ Clearly and regularly communicate individual and collective expectations. Use every channel available to be sure that every person and every team "gets the new picture". We need to deliver a message between 3 and 7 times *on average* for it to have a shot at being understood accurately and turned into action. And that's just the average. If expectations are muddy or uneven, confusing, inconsistent and wide open for interpretation, don't expect the results to be clean, crisp and on target.

✪ Assist each person to appreciate the specific role they play, the functions they perform and the duties and responsibilities that come with them. Devote the time and energy to make this important connection with those around you. How is the guy scrubbing the pots clean in the cafeteria contributing to the organization's success? The janitor? The law clerk? Tell them what you see through your leadership lens and watch them walk away with their swagger on!

✪ Create universal knowledge and understanding of the "bright line boundaries" within the organization. These might include: codes of conduct, ground rules, behavioral norms, performance standards, best practices and organizational procedures. We all need to know and follow the rules of the organization. No surprise that this is at the top of the list of what we expect from capable, well-intended adults at work. Know the code and choose accordingly!

✪ Define and clearly communicate the consequences of exceeding or falling short of expectations. None of us is perfect. There will be times when we miss the mark. We've got to make it our business to know and accept the consequences of our choices (and not making a choice is a choice). It's equally important to understand what happens when we go above and beyond.

There's one more item on the list of accountability prerequisites. This is the pinch point for many organizations. This item can make or break our efforts to create an environment of accountability:

✪ Transparently develop and follow a system that fairly and courageously applies those natural consequences to the adult choices that are made. Too often we lack the organizational will to apply the consequences to the choices that people make; when rules have been broken and expectations are unmet. We look the other way; bend those rules; make idle threats; give fourth and fifth chances. Expectations are meaningless without consequences.

Taken together, these macro-level basics forge a framework and begin to create the conditions that will allow accountability to grow into our way of life at work. Take another, more thoughtful look over this list. Which of these does your organization already do very well? Place a check by those. Which of these are not done at all or not done well? Give them an asterisk.

Remember our earlier stone wall exercise? The absence of these accountability prerequisites are often what blocks us from achieving the level of accountability that we want and need. If the basics aren't in place to ground the organization, then creating an accountability culture will be much tougher; some might even argue impossible.

You might be thinking that you don't have much influence over these big picture, organizational items so they're someone else's responsibility. Not so fast! First, you may have more influence than you think. Challenge that way of thinking about yourself. Second, if your influence is truly limited, then you need to focus on those things over which you do exert some control.

You need to do what you can from your seat to make sure that these basics are in place. Don't forget that you own the success of the whole organization! Get used to "choosing accountability" by starting right now to change your mindset.

Be warned, you haven't heard the last of these basics. In the following chapters we'll move to the micro-level by identifying small picture actions that you can take to be accountable and to help others to also choose accountability. The idea is to always reinforce the big picture.

Maybe there's some truth to the old adage: take care of the small things and the big things will take care of themselves!

PART TWO

Accountability: What It's All About

HIGHLIGHTS

Orienting Toward the Positive

- ✪ We cannot "hold others accountable."
- ✪ Compliance is different than personal accountability.
- ✪ Each of us can do what we can from where we are. That means working at the "small picture" or micro-level to reinforce the big picture basics.

Finding Your Way to Accountability

- ✪ The definition of personal accountability is simple but powerful: Doing the right thing consistently, day after day, in both task and relationships to live the mission and values of the organization and advance its vision.

- ✪ We must adopt the **The Accountability Credo**

  - ★ We are a group of capable adults.
  - ★ Most people want to do credible work.
  - ★ We ultimately choose or decide how to be at work.
  - ★ Accountability is an adult choice.
  - ★ Our shared responsibility is to co-create environmental conditions that foster & reward that choice.

- ✪ We must assure that the following Accountability Pre-requisites (or Big Picture Basics) are securely in place in our organization.

  - ★ Universal (yes, that means absolutely everyone!) knowledge and understanding of the vision, mission, values, strategies and goals of the organization AND help everyone to make the connection between them and the choices they make each day at work.

★ Define accountability in simple, straightforward terms that a 12 year old would understand.

★ Clearly and regularly communicate individual and collective expectations.

★ Assist each person to appreciate the specific role they play, the functions they perform and the duties and responsibilities that come with them.

★ Create universal knowledge and understanding of the "bright line boundaries" within the organization.

★ Define and clearly communicate the consequences of exceeding or falling short of expectations.

★ Transparently develop and follow a system that fairly and courageously applies those natural consequences to the adult choices that are made.

If you've successfully worked through Part One and have thoughtfully considered Part Two, then you're well positioned and, hopefully, eager to roll up your sleeves, deepen your understanding of what's at the core of accountability and replace stale habits of thought, belief and behavior with a fresh set by crafting new accountability conversations and co-creating accountability partnerships. This work comes with a warning label: it involves both learning and un-learning. Both come with a desire to know more and a willingness to do the work no matter how uncomfortable it may seem at the time. It requires both grit and gusto from each of us.

But I invite you to stick with it, because the rewards, for both you and your organization have the potential to take your breath away. The virtuous cycle captured in the **Accountability Compass** shows us the way to create a *conspiracy of goodness* within our teams and our organization. The first time that I came across this power phrase—a conspiracy of goodness—was in a story about a small French mountain village, Le Chambon-sur-Lignon. The entire town took the great risk to quietly shelter five-thousand Jews during the Nazi occupation of France. They were ordinary people, often poverty stricken themselves, doing the right thing day in and day for, not days, but for years! And not one Jewish person was lost.

Now, admittedly, our work of accountability may not be of this same magnitude or consequence; but that doesn't mean that it is any less worthy. We too must be courageous and tenacious. And we must be committed to doing the right thing for the longer term. I genuinely believe that this work can change lives and create a healthier, more vibrant organizational energy. Take the leadership dare and read on!

PART
THREE

CHOOSE ACCOUNTABILITY TOGETHER!

6

The Look and Feel of a Culture of Accountability

Personal accountability requires a daily dose of a potent cocktail of intentionality, resolve, resilience and verve. There is no magic wand or fairy dust to make it happen. An accountability-rich culture is made up of adults who choose to do the right thing in lots of small ways each day.

Here is an example of how something could have gone very wrong but ultimately went exactly the way we would like it to go—all because someone was willing to *Own It!*

> *Almost all of us have had the experience of untangling a credit card snafu. I don't know about your batting average, but mine is less than .500 in getting my outcome of choice.*
>
> *Consider Renee's situation. She has been a happy, satisfied customer of a well-known national retailer. In fact, she was so loyal that she decided to take advantage of a special offer and apply for their credit card. Difficulties began the very first time that she used the card. She paid her bill on time, only to find that the next bill had an illegitimate late charge assessed on her account. She dutifully called the sponsoring bank and was told that it had been removed.*
>
> *The next month an additional late fee was assessed despite having no additional purchases AND the original late fee had not been removed. Renee's second call to the bank was less cordial, but they agreed to wipe the slate clean. The*

final straw for Renee was the threatening collection call she received from the bank. They demanded payment and used strong bullying language and tactics. Exasperated, Renee paid the fees and closed her account, vowing never to do business with the bank and the retailer again!

Talk about the wrong thing to do. Bad for the retailer. Bad for the bank's reputation. And bad for Renee. The saddest part is that it didn't have to be that way. Hard to believe that this story has an uplifting ending; but it actually does. In fact, it stands as a stellar example of a commitment to accountability. Read on…

Renee was so frustrated that she actually visited her local retailer in person to share this disturbing story and let them know that she would no longer shop there. The manager, Jess, fielded this animated, angry customer complaint in the store. Although Jess had no direct authority over the credit card company, or even any interaction with it because it was a third-party vendor, she nonetheless, listened skillfully, asked great questions, offered specific suggestions on remedies and validated Renee. She spent time with her and made sure she apologized for the experience. Jesse did the right thing even though she and her team had nothing to do with the problem.

She told me later that such experiences color the perception of their entire company and it is her role to repair that! She gets it—no matter who was responsible, she made it her problem and solved it. In addition to giving Renee concrete suggestions on how to lodge a complaint and get reconsideration, Jesse also gave the customer a very generous amount of "in store cash" to make it right. This "cash" was far in excess of the amount the client paid in late fees. Finally, Jess asked for Renee's contact information so that she could call her to see how things went for her. WOW!

Did Renee remain a customer of that store? I think you know the answer. All hail the power of doing the right thing!

I interact with organizations in many different ways in the course of my professional work and my personal life. Regardless of whether I'm wearing my coach's hat or that of educator, speaker, author or even "customer," I want to feel assured that accountability is increasingly an integral part of the framework for doing business or that the organization and team members are ready to work toward that goal; that each organizational citizen is doing her/his individual part to "own it!" both with the big and little "stuff."

When I see and experience examples of accountability, I have confidence and trust in that organization's ability to be successful in the longer term. However, I also know there is much work to do in this arena because I often work with organizations as significant gaps in accountability are addressed and reduced.

Part Three is all about how I work with organizations to foster and sustain accountability as a non-negotiable individual and collective requirement. When accountability is embedded in the spirit of an organization, here's what it looks and feels like:

Most of us accept broad personal responsibility for the success of the entire organization. Even if that means helping others with their work; working cross-functionally to provide better service or doing tasks that aren't technically "in our job description." Throughout our day, we seize any moment to make things right for the people we serve and for one another. We operate each day as though our name is on the sign out front!

✪ What does this sound like in everyday communication?

"How can I help you? I know you're swamped and I have a few extra minutes" or

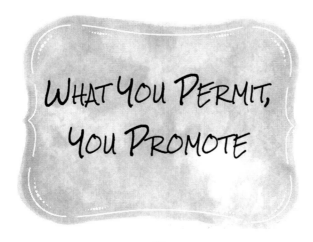

WHAT YOU PERMIT, YOU PROMOTE

"How can our departments work together more seamlessly? This rivalry has gone on far too long!"

"Moving patients from the Emergency Department to an inpatient unit is a priority for us all, not just the ED. We all need to be part of the solution so that our patients have a safe and positive experience."

✪ Individually, most of us understand that we are the eyes, ears, heart and voice of the organization. What we choose to say or do in any of the hundreds of interactions we may have with those who are important to our success is consequential.

For example, we pick up the trash at the entrance to our building, not because we are members of the janitorial staff, but because we know that our janitors cannot be everywhere at once and leaving the trash there will only reflect unfavorably on us all. We want our clients/customers to have the best overall impression of our organization possible.

✪ Most of us look within ourselves to find the discipline and the will to manage our own morale (or energy level), commitment and motivation. Because we act as capable adults, there is little need for an external pressure to force us to comply or manage these things for us.

✪ Most of us choose to lead from our seats! We take our work seriously. We understand how that work interconnects with others' work and how it contributes to the success of the organization. We are constructive and generally positive.

✪ Most of us make it our business to own the moment! We show up as the best version of ourselves each day. We realize that the little stuff matters when it comes to accountability.

For example, we own responsibility for the success of each meeting that we attend. And we demonstrate that personal responsibility by being well prepared for those meetings; helping the facilitator to be successful; being fully engaged; clearly listening to others; staying fully awake and alert; and finding our voices to share our thoughts when necessary.

✪ Most of us know the rules and guidelines and choose to follow them, regardless of whether or not the boss is present. We do it because it's the adult thing to do and the right thing to do.

✪ Most of us extend a spirit of goodwill, civility and respect to our colleagues. We choose to think the best of others until there is evidence to the contrary. We practice the Platinum Rule—treating others as they would like to be treated. Ours is a welcoming spirit.

✪ Most of us bravely confront gaps in accountability in group settings. We speak up when others are avoiding accountability. We have difficult conversations with others, particularly when the stakes are high. We realize that when we remain silent witnesses to less than accountable behaviors, we are actually signaling those involved that we approve at some level. (Think of Hanna's story when you see, feel, or hear of this happening, and remember how badly that turned out).

The Accountability Mantra

As we move into the various actions and tactics that we can use to co-create an accountability-rich culture, we already know that there will be road blocks and resistance—both internal (inside your own self) and externally (outside forces in your organization that may not want change or are very uncomfortable with it.) Remember the stone wall?

There is one simple phrase that I have come across in many different arenas and from many different sources (so many that I have no idea who originally said it). It reminds us of this dynamic and challenges any dysfunctional comfort that we may have. If you don't remember anything else that I have written about in this book, commit this to heart: What you permit you promote!

I call it the "accountability mantra," because it offers a forceful reminder that our inaction to address unacceptable behaviors can, and often will, be interpreted as *permission by others to continue to do the wrong thing*. I invite you to allow this simple yet powerful phrase to be your personal reminder to practice accountability, one decision, one action at a time and to do what you can to help others around you to make the same choice.

Don't Be the Weakest Link

I'm encouraging you to keep that accountability mantra top of mind because to choose otherwise is a costly mistake.

We're probably all familiar with the maxim in mechanics that the weakest link in a chain is a measure of the strength of the whole. In business terms, that translates to the notion that an organization is only as powerful as its weakest person. In fact, the person who's making the least contribution to the collective achievement of the team is sometimes called, "the weakest link."

Some of you might associate this term with a short lived television game show, *The Weakest Link*. At various turning points in the game, the host would shrilly call out—Mary....you are the weakest link! And the humiliated contestant would slink off the stage as he/she exited the game.

Culturally, we operate as an *accountability chain*. We are an interlocked system of individuals and teams, linked in mutual support in order to achieve something that's meaningful, and each expected to demonstrate personal accountability to make that happen. When the majority chooses to habitually do the right thing, our chain is strong and allows us to get truly remarkable things accomplished together. On the other hand, when some don't hold themselves accountable, *the entire collective effort is jeopardized.* Additional pressure is placed on other "links" in the chain. Eventually the chain breaks. The project fails. We miss our goals. Processes break down.

> *Mark was a new team member at a large customer service call center. He joined a table full of his colleagues in the break room one afternoon. They were making fun of another colleague (who wasn't present). The comments were pretty harsh. Mark had to admit that the person who was the subject of this stinging gossip was pretty quirky. But he sort of liked him; and they were becoming friendly.*
>
> *Mark wanted to stand up for this guy or at least change the subject and move the conversation in another direction. But he also wanted to be accepted by this group of peers. And, in the end, he wanted to fit in more than he wanted to do*

the right thing. He said nothing and by his silence he sent a
message of approval to the group.

I can only imagine what happened to that "other colleague," and I doubt that call center routinely enjoys high levels of engagement and talent retention.

Making the choice to "do the right thing" can test the strength of relationships, and you may feel alone at times. But ask yourself, what kind of world do we live in where somehow it's okay to condone behavior that is definitely "not right," in service of "keeping the peace," or saving a friendship, or whatever?

> *Marisol's friend at work, was running late and called to ask*
> *Marisol to punch in for her so that she would not be charged*
> *with a late arrival. Marisol really wanted to do this favor for*
> *her friend because she had been so supportive when Marisol's*
> *Mom died. But she knew it was dishonest. Instead, Marisol*
> *decided to tell the Supervisor that her friend was on her*
> *way but was running just a few minutes late and offered to*
> *cover the friend's work until she arrived. Even though the*
> *friend did not get in trouble for being late, she was angry*
> *that Marisol did not do what she asked. She "unfriended"*
> *her at work and spoke negatively about her to other team*
> *members. Marisol is feeling isolated now and wonders if she*
> *did the right thing --She did!*

As adults we need to understand that our everyday choices don't just affect us individually. There are significant implications for our team and our entire organization and we need to act accordingly. Do you really want to be "the weakest link"?

Accountability Inventory

In 1961, Joan Didion, a well-known literary journalist and American cultural critic, wrote an essay for *Vogue* magazine that made her readers take a hard look at themselves in the mirror. Called "On Self-Respect," it was written to fill the space in the magazine left void by another writer who failed to make the deadline. Later published in her first book *Slouching Towards Bethlehem*, it became one of Didion's seminal pieces. It demanded the reader ask themselves the hard questions about their actions in the cold, lonely dark of night, when no one was around to make them feel better about themselves if they had done something that compromised their "self-respect," their ability to hold themselves accountable.[11]

It's time for you to take an honest, courageous look in the leadership mirror and ask the million dollar question: Are you personally accountable at work? Here's a simple tool that can help you to find your answer.

Personal Accountability Inventory

Read each statement thoughtfully. If you believe that a statement is true of you most of the time, then check the box next to that statement. If not, leave it blank. When you are finished, eyeball your responses. This isn't a test so there's no scoring and no grade. A careful look will tell you all you need to know about how well you live personal accountability at work.

_____	**Do you bring an owner's mentality to your job?**
_____	**Do you do what's right instead of what's easy?**
_____	**Can you be counted on almost 100 percent of the time?**
_____	**Are you willing to admit a mistake?**
_____	**Are you willing to correct a mistake even if it was not your fault?**
_____	**Do you arrive on time almost every day?**
_____	**Do you rarely, if ever, miss a scheduled day of work?**

---

11   Joan Didion. *Slouching Towards Bethlehem.* New York: Farrar, Straus and Giroux. 1961. Print.

_____ **Do you meet deadlines?**

_____ **Are you regularly part of the solution rather than part of the problem?**

_____ **Do you regularly exceed expectations?**

_____ **Do you make it an everyday habit to help your team mates and your boss?**

_____ **Do you make it your personal responsibility to keep your projects and assignments on track from start to finish—leading from your seat to resolve challenges?**

_____ **Do you put in a full day's work each day?**

_____ **Do you broadly define your individual accountability to include accountability for the success of your team AND the whole organization?**

_____ **When you identify a problem, do you come up with a solution?**

_____ **Do you speak and act with goodwill, civility and respect almost always?**

_____ **Do you resolve differences by talking directly with the other person(s)?**

_____ **Do you regularly offer ideas on how to do your work better and differently?**

_____ **Do you accept change gracefully?**

_____ **Do you have a winning attitude most days?**

Because we are now moving into the challenging work of co-creating an ongoing culture of accountability, it's even more important to gather our thoughts and ideas. As we did in Part One and Two, I am offering you space to write down inspired actions that occur to you as you read. These can be new ideas or upgrades you want to make to your everyday language, in all your interactions and relationships in your work life.

Gather Your Thoughts—What insights did you gain from completing the Inventory? Did any of the questions surprise you? What will you do differently as a result?

_____

_____

_____

_____

Organizational Accountability Inventory

Because we form a chain of accountability through the interrelatedness of our work, every person in an organization must do his or her part to co-create an environment that fosters, rewards and ultimately requires personal accountability at all levels and across all functional areas.

Here is an organizational inventory that can spark important discussions within your organization. It can serve as an accountability checkpoint for an entire organization or a specific division, department or unit.

Directions: Read each statement thoughtfully. If you believe that a statement is true of your organization most of the time, then check the box next to that statement. If not, leave it blank. When you are finished, review your own responses and discuss them with others. This isn't a test so there's no scoring and no grade. Instead, it offers insight into current best practices. A careful look will tell you all you need to know about whether your organization's culture is dominated by a strong sense of personal accountability.

_____ **Does your organization have a clear, written definition of accountability that is known by all?**

_____ **Is your organization's cultural commitment to personal accountability discussed in detail during the onboarding process for new team members?**

_____ **Does your organization have an accountability commitment statement that is signed by each team member, no exceptions?**

_____	Is the accountability commitment statement reviewed and re-signed annually?
_____	Does your organization offer at least one required educational program on accountability?
_____	Does your boss regularly have conversations of accountability with you and your team mates, both individually and as a team?
_____	Are team members encouraged to talk to one another about perceived gaps in accountability?
_____	Does your boss take action to address gaps in accountability?
_____	Is there universal understanding of the consequences of not acting as an accountable adult at work?
_____	Are the consequences applied fairly and consistently within the organization?
_____	Does your organization regularly recognize "accountability role models"—those who faithfully practice personal accountability?

Gather Your Thoughts—What insights did you gain from completing the Inventory? Did any of the questions surprise you? What will you do differently as a result? With whom have you shared this Inventory? How can you use it strategically to begin a new conversation within your organization?

_____

_____

_____

_____

Accountability TO GO

Our commitment as everyday leaders must go well beyond reading about accountability; we've got to run with what we learn, even when it's uncomfortable and activate the learning in a meaningful way in our experience. So let's import what we've learned and take action to change. Let's box it up and take it TO GO!

Here are some suggestions to get out of the gate. Add your own actions to mine and you've just started your very own action plan.

1. Make the Accountability Credo an everyday mantra. Share it with colleagues. Discuss it at staff meetings. Make it a part of your department's on-boarding rituals. Align your behaviors behind it. For example, do you treat your colleagues as capable adults each day?

2. Practice holding yourself accountable for the success of the entire organization. If you owned your organization (the plant, the bank, the hospital, the grocery store, etc.) what would you be doing that you're not doing today? Or, what would you stop doing that you're doing today? How would you feel as you walked into the building?

3. Take the Accountability Inventory. Take it seriously. Take it to heart. Make some changes. Ask others to take it. Talk about it together.

4. Remove the phrase, "hold others accountable" from your vocabulary. Stop yourself when tempted to use it. It only reinforces a myth about accountability.

5. Find out if your organization has its own definition of accountability. Learn it. Compare it to the one you developed and the one I offered. How is it different? Better? How can it be improved? No definition? You know what to do about that!

6. Lead a discussion of the phrase—**What you permit, you promote**—with your team mates.

7. Take the organizational accountability inventory. Encourage others to do the same. Discuss it with your boss, your People (Human Resources) Executive and other thought leaders. Is the organization doing its part to create and sustain a culture of accountability? Where are the pinch points? Identify a quick win?

7

Step Up and Be a Coach Leader

The "new normal" of engaged organizations that foster cultures of accountability doesn't just happen by happy accident very often if ever; it happens intentionally. It must rely on and be nurtured by a model or approach that offers each of us, regardless of position, the opportunity, confidence, and know how to engage as an owner; as a leader.

While there are other workable options, the model I find to be the best fit is "coach leadership." From my years of experience bearing witness to individual and cultural transformations, I am wholeheartedly convinced that significant change is only possible when the individual and/or the organization is willing and committed to creating a rock solid foundation on which to build a new way of working. Only when we truly understand the changing nature of leadership and its pivotal link to full-throttle engagement at work AND put that new understanding into practice day after day, will we be ready to choose accountability individually and collectively. Coach leadership is that coalescing practice.

This chapter offers a skinny version of the comprehensive overview of the coach leader model and the skills it demands that is provided in *Volume 1, Take The Lead.* If you've already read it, consider this a tune-up. If you haven't, consider this a preview that will jump start your ability to practice and sustain personal accountability.

Being a Coach

The first point is to understand what I mean by coaching and the work a coach does in any organization.

Coaching is an intentionally designed system for change based on communication that is results-oriented and stokes passion by removing obstacles to our success. By its very nature it helps create the environment where the everyday leader is able to take charge of his or her work and thrive as a result.

And before anyone starts to protest, I'm here to set the record straight about the fierce potential that a universal leadership approach rooted in the coaching tradition has to change our work lives for good and forever. Think about it. Coaching is a long-standing, well-respected, even sacred tradition of one person helping another to be at their best. Influencers from all disciplines have used coaching as a powerful ally to exceed their goals.

So *forget what you think you know about coaching!* Don't allow that one bad experience with someone calling themselves a coach to color your opinion and wall you off from some of the most worthwhile learning of your life.

Set aside the following popular mis-conceptions that float around about coaching:

- ✪ Coaching is just an intervention when someone makes a mistake
- ✪ It's for "losers"
- ✪ Coaching is for sissies—it means that you're weak and ineffective
- ✪ It's a cool new label for the same-old, same-old disciplinary process of "writing people up"
- ✪ It's a twisted version of I'm okay-you're okay, therefore anything goes at work.

Instead, return with me to the roots of coaching. At its core, coaching is a directed conversation with oneself and with others that is aimed at helping, growing, and challenging. It is purposeful and skillful. It's about meaningful relationships. It's gutsy and results-driven because it requires everyone to be willing to tell the truth and find their own solutions—even to very difficult situations. It's edgy. It is the polar opposite of the old command and control model. One of the fundamental assumptions of the coaching tradition is that almost all people are capable, willing, creative, and bright *adults*. Coaching demands that everyone lead from their seat. The good news is that anyone can do it and it can be applied to all situations at work.

Allow me to be especially plainspoken for a moment. The coaching framework and its accompanying language offer a channel to reimagine, reinvent, reengineer, and then to revive our workplaces. Coaching is the energy conductor for raising the level of engagement and *creating leaders in every seat*. Coaching means that we believe in and then work toward bringing out the very best in ourselves and then others; this includes our boss, the boss's boss, our peers, our teammates, and those who may call us boss.

Coach Leadership is the essence of engagement and the foundation of accountability.

The Essence of Coach Leadership

To become an accountability-rich culture, where the Accountability Compass is in constant use, guiding us to ever more success, we need to universally adopt and master the coach leader approach to our relationships, our work and our customers. The mental model, the assumptions and the language of coaching directly fuels, even turbo charges, personal accountability! It's that simple and straightforward. So, if you want to reach that new level of accountability for yourself and help others around you to do the same, you need to be a coach leader.

Coach leadership is different than managing and/or directing people, *and* it offers the primary route for all of us to lead from our seats and practice full-throttle engagement. By its very nature, the coaching model requires that we routinely act as capable, accountable adults and expect that others will as well. Coach leadership is one of the most powerful and potent approaches for organizations wanting to create and sustain the embedded cultural value of accountability! *So, then, what exactly is it?* What are the key distinctions that make it so different and so useful in creating fully engaged, accountable workplaces?

Here is my simple definition of coach leadership:

> *Coach leadership is a way of interacting with another (or others) that promotes improvement and development. In other words, it brings about or contributes to positive change, primarily through the will of the other person(s) rather than simply out of obedience to me or you or even "them." Great*

coach leaders believe wholeheartedly that there is brilliance in everyone and they understand just as wholeheartedly that the primary responsibility of coach leaders is to assist others in accessing their own brilliances, their own answers, and then taking inspired action from there to get the work done well. When practiced more and more universally in an organization, by more and more people at more and more levels, coach leadership is the fuel that powers full-throttle engagement. And this fuel is completely renewable and resides in abundant supply within all of us.

While coach leadership is quite simple, it is not at all easy for many of us to carry in our head, heart, and gut day in and day out because it has not been our habit to do so. It requires a significant shift in our individual and team patterns. It definitely takes lots of unlearning and involves a good measure of risk taking and belief. Above all, it takes tenacity to keep it going when things inevitably get tough.

It is so powerful and so effective because, at its core, it is a fundamental belief that the other person is a capable, smart, and talented adult willing to contribute. Coach leadership rides on the firm belief that the person who is closest to the actual work often "knows best," which means that they have the answers to the problem they face; they just need the space in which to find it, express it, and put it into action.

As coach leaders, we must hold the other person in "unconditional positive regard," a marvelous phrase coined by Thomas Crane.[12] The primary gift of coach leadership is the embedded challenge to create our own solutions. To accomplish that, everyone needs the permission and the space to allow that to happen. Decision making is de-centralized and pushed throughout the organization to absolutely everyone.

Stop for a moment and truly consider the implications of that claim. The gift of coach leadership is that it promotes an organizational culture in which everyone routinely is an everyday leader, leading powerfully and fully from their seat.

One of my favorite quotes captures this so perfectly:

---

12   Thomas G, Crane. *The Heart of Coaching* (San Diego, CA: FTA Press, 2005. Page 39.

Change done by me is an opportunity.
Change done to me is a threat.
All change looks like failure in the middle.

Rosabeth Moss Kanter

Coach leadership feels like "change done by me" more often than not because it calls on each of us to make decisions, to be active problem solvers and take charge adults, rather than passive "Stepford-like" human resources. More stuff gets done "by me" and that is an opportunity. Coaching happens inside relationships, in real conversations between *success partners*. Instead of telling or directing or "bossing" someone around, coaching demands that we create solutions and move forward through *collaborative inquiry* (sometimes called appreciative inquiry) which means that we are working together to ask the right questions that will lead to viable solutions.

As coach leaders, we coach with rather than to. We ask and answer high quality questions together aimed at accessing options, alternatives, fresh perspectives, laser focused insights, and BFOs (blinding flashes of the obvious). Coaching is an effective way of being together at *all* levels within an organization and in *all* interactions. As coach leaders, we want the best for each of our colleagues as much as we want that for ourselves. By its very nature, it creates leaders around you at all levels and layers of the organization.

In order to be effective as coach leaders, all people in the dialogue both teach and learn in the rhythm of everyday conversations. In this type of situation, *everyone* understands that there will be times when they take the lead and there will be times when they follow someone else's lead. Coach leadership cracks open the door for some of the most productive brainstorming I've ever witnessed because it is done collaboratively (yes, there's that word again). Everyone is included in strategy, planning, and goal setting.

As coach leaders, those with traditional leadership titles challenge their team members to find their own solutions, take charge of projects or tasks, and go beyond the average. The traditional leader learns how to get out the way and let their team members step up and take responsibility for the work that's been handed to them. For that effort, the traditional leader rewards independent and innovative thinking and behaving; they are willing to share power and authority. And they get the importance of celebrating. These leaders stop acting like parents, wardens, know it alls, or dictators.

When universal coach leadership is practiced, staff members and/or team members step up. They stop waiting to be told what to do. They take risks by offering solutions, speaking up, and telling the truth. They become constructive, going well beyond the minimum. They stop acting like children, victims, cynics, and I-told-you-so's.

At the most fundamental level of language, coaching is not about "I" or "you" or "them" but about "we." We assist each other in identifying obstacles so as to move more easily and quickly around them and get on with the business of co-creating a great place to work. We collectively keep our eyes on the overall good of the entire organization instead of a narrow focus on getting our tasks done. We ask questions and listen in order to expand our perspectives and surface up more and different solutions and new opportunities. We keep the focus to insure success.

There is a saying that is often attributed to Lao Tzu: "Feed a man a fish, feed him for a day. Teach him how to fish and feed him for a lifetime." Coach leadership is closely aligned with the latter. If we assist one another to have the courage and the will to look within for solutions; if we get out of each other's way so that we can take chances, learn, grow, and lead, then we will stand a much improved chance of having what we say we all want: an engaged, energetic workforce; a team who holds themselves accountable with peak performance and the results to prove it.

In this way, you can view coach leadership as a way of being and acting, something that is:

- ✪ All about change.
- ✪ Moving from where we are today to where we want to be next.
- ✪ An organic, holistic process—not a gimmick, not the program of the month, and certainly not an "intervention" for troubled employees.
- ✪ Used by everyone. It is 360-degrees around the organization— coaching up, down, and across in an organization. But it is also coaching within by skillfully coaching ourselves.

✪ Based on a powerful belief that each of us has almost all of the answers within us and that what we need to access them is a success partner who believes in us and can assist us in holding the frame of possibility.

Coach leadership is as much about unlearning as it is about learning. Businesses in the know gravitate towards it because it is absolutely results driven. Any "coaching" resource that says otherwise isn't coaching. Coach leadership challenges. It demands the best. It's edgy and risky. It's big and bold.

Coaching offers a platform for surfacing up limiting beliefs, old programs, and patterns and allows us to shift them. To do that requires us to connect not just to logic, but to intuitive intelligence and emotional intelligence as well.

When it's done well, coach leadership becomes a portal for adding incredible clarity and vision to one's work because it is supported by built-in accountability.

Coach Leader Commitments

Coach leaders have what the Buddhists call "crazy wisdom." The way that I understand this idea is a unique blend of wisdom, storytelling/drama, and boldness. I encourage each of you to rejoice and "re-choice" each day in "being" a coach leader in your workplace. For me that involves, at a minimum, making a daily commitment to *be*:

✪ **An intentional communicator**—Choose your words, your tone of voice, and your body language carefully. Pause before speaking and consider how best to deliver a message that will help you, your colleagues and your organization to be at their best.

✪ **Non-judgmental**—Do not rush to judge others. Be intentional about your feelings and remain neutral. Think the best of others. Decide how you will choose to feel knowing that how you feel will, at least in part, determine how things will go.

✪ **An ego tamer**—Choose to help others be at their best; choose to make a contribution to their greatness; and choose to bring your best self to work for the good of the organization not simply to make yourself look good. While I believe that it is helpful to have a healthy ego and to appreciate ourselves, it does not always have to be about us.

✪ **Open to new possibilities and options**—As coach leaders, we come to recognize that our way of thinking and being is not the only game in town. We begin to value diversity of thought as a critical factor in creativity, innovation, and continuous quality improvement. If we all thought alike, wouldn't things be boring! We become willing to try new ways of doing things. We entertain the idea that we may not have the whole picture. Even though we have done it "our way" a million times, we are at peace with a new level of understanding there is more than one acceptable way to get us where we need to be.

✪ **Focused on signature strengths**—Coach leadership is a strength- or "brilliance-" based approach to relationships at work. As a coach, we are called upon to uncover and then uplift our own strengths or brilliances as well as the brilliances of others. Eighty percent of time, energy, and attention should be focused on knowing and then growing our own and others' brilliances. Only 20 percent of our attention should be focused on what I call lesser strengths (you probably call them weaknesses). To bring out the best in ourselves and others, we must concentrate on what's great about us and them and then accentuate that in all that they do.

✪ **Willing to surrender the need to "fix" someone or be fixed by someone else**—we are here to support, uplift, and believe in our colleagues. But they are in charge of themselves; we cannot control others. We are only in charge of us! So, focus there and allow others to do their own mastery work. Hold others big in their experience; have high expectations; at the same time, realize that this must be a choice that they intentionally make. The work is still theirs to do. WE must adopt the approach that we and everyone is "perfect enough" where they are today. We are all on our individual life journeys and we need to honor the fact that we can all be in different places. That does not make anyone wrong or inferior, just at a different spot in their evolution of thought.

✪ **Willing to surrender the outcome**—This can be a challenge for some of us, even more so than some of the other daily commitments to "being" a coach leader. Surrendering the outcome simply calls upon us to give up the notion that there is only one way (typically our way) to get something accomplished well. Allow others to offer and then attempt different approaches. Do so, not from a place of hoping that they fail and prove that you were right after all, but rather because you want that person(s) to be successful in their own right.

✪ **Results oriented, not a results machine**—It is not only about the outcome, the destination or the result. The process, the journey is also important. In it resides much learning and growing, excitement and fun, and the opportunity to do good work together. Of course we all want successes; I want them for you. But I frequently challenge my clients by saying that I, as a coach leader, would prefer a bold failure over a mediocre success. Let's not play it too safe; let's try new approaches because that's the innovative process in action. Savor the journey as well as the destination.

✪ **The "Poster Adult" for the Accountability Credo**—At our core, coach leaders must believe that their colleagues are a group of capable adults and that most of them want to do good work and make a difference. Coach leaders choose to be personally accountable every day. Not simply when it's convenient or on "good hair" days or when things are going smoothly.

In summary, here is what goes through the coach leader's mind as s/he approaches each new day: *I can and should coach all day and every day to everyone with whom I interact. That means that I coach myself, my team-mates, my boss, others in my organization, and even those who are my clients, customers, or patients. In fact, if I choose to expand my thinking even further, I can and should coach my family, friends, and community. I can and should coach because it feels good to me and to others; it has the potential to bring out the best in others and it positions my organization and my community for maximum positive results. Built into its framework is the requirement to "do the right thing in both task and relationship." I am a coach leader. It is my way of being, rather than an intervention. In fact, it has become such a part of who I am, that I never have to say the words, "let me coach you."*

Coaching Starter Kit

These are the foundational coaching skills that, when practiced faithfully day in and day out, are guaranteed to allow you to lead from your seat; improve your relationships; promote accountability; foster higher levels of engagement; and ultimately result to better service to your customers/clients/patients and overall success. They include:

- ✪ **Coach Leader Behavior #1:** Faithfully practice engaged, clear listening.

- ✪ **Coach Leader Behavior #2:** Choose words with great care (intentional languaging).

- ✪ **Coach Leader Behavior #3:** Be aware of nonverbal messaging and make sensible choices that help (intentional nonverbal communication).

If these skills seem simple to you, well, you're right. They are simple; but not easy to do day in and day out. If you want to change your organizational culture, then change the conversation.

To change the culture...Change the conversation

Peter Block

Don't make the novice mistake of discounting the power of these skills. Together, they form the backbone of conversational intelligence. If you genuinely want an accountability-rich culture, this coaching starter kit will put you on the right track.

Coach Leader Behavior #1:
Faithfully Practice Engaged, Clear Listening

There is no better gift that we could bestow on our colleagues, teammates, clients, and our organizations than to become a more engaged, clear listener. In fact, there is no more impactful gift that we can give ourselves.

Listening is the very essence, the soul, of coach leadership. It has the potential in and of itself to be transformative because it provides us an ideal chance to learn and discover. Through engaged, clear listening, we get to send our curiosity on a mission.

Fully engaged listening means bringing the "full monty" of yourself to an exchange. You are present in the moment, undistracted, and attentive. Clear listening means that we are open and curious about learning and absorbing everything from the dialogue. It doesn't assume that we must immediately analyze or judge what we're hearing. Engaged, clear listening can yield disproportionate results when compared to the effort involved. You will be so much wiser, connected, and alive; so much more aware and attuned to the people and the environment around you.

Shakespeare dares us in King Lear to, "Look with thine ears." Research supports the power of engaged, clear listening. Study after study affirms that 9 out of 10 (90 percent) employee problems stem from someone not feeling heard!

Despite all of this evidence, listening is still rarely taught at any educational level. It relies primarily on emotional and intuitive intelligence and, for this reason, has often been undervalued in the Industrial and even in the Information Ages' organizational and leadership models. In those eras, we required professionals to have strong writing skills. Excellent oral communication skills were emphasized and highly sought after. Today listening is fast becoming a value-added strength in business. Get ready for it. Tom Peters believes that the "single most strategic strength that an organization can cultivate, is a commitment to listening on the part of every member of the organization."[13]

Do you consider yourself, today, at work, an extraordinary listener? When I ask audiences to think about that question and honestly answer it, only a handful has a strong conviction that they possess above-average skill in this area. Even fewer have made it a priority to take an educational program focused entirely on listening. And I must acknowledge that this level of listening is more challenging for some communication styles; it does not come as naturally to some as others. If we are to become coach leaders and assist ourselves, our colleagues, and our organizations to be the best

---

13   Tom Peters Video. "Listening." TomPeters.com. http://www.youtube.com/watch?v=lwB7NAvKPeo.

that we/they can be, then we must *resolve* to consistently be an extraordinary listener. In my opinion, there is nothing else that you can do that will advantage your team more than practicing engaged, clear listening.

Let's connect our heart, head, and gut and embrace this learning with gusto. I want to share my seven secrets to listening with a coach leader's ear. I will promise you that if you wholeheartedly make these your habits, your experiences will be transformed over time!

Developing a coach leader's ear

1. **Practice silence—**

The first and most potent step toward more engaged listening is to practice silence regularly. There are two aspects of silence that deserve our attention. First, in order to make room to listen, we must quiet all of the thoughts that are competing for our mind's attention. On average, Americans have about sixty-thousand thoughts each day; most are what is generally considered negative and repetitive.[14]

Because listening is an inspired action, we need to focus our attention on the listening instead of sharing our attention with many, many thoughts and also attempting to listen. Now, I know that many of us have become avid multitaskers. Here is an important question: is multitasking the most effective way of getting things done effectively at work? The answer is no. In fact, studies have shown that we lose ten IQ points when we are attempting to multitask (we do get them back when we stop!). And recent studies have suggested that it is impossible to actually multitask. This begs the question, why try?

Yes, I know that we can do basic functions such as walking and talking at the same time. But when it comes to developing and tending to relationships and being a part of workplace conversations, I am encouraging you to "single handle" the act of listening. This means to pay undivided attention to the other person(s). Quiet your "head trash," all of those other thoughts flying through your mind. Gently, easily do your best to just listen. Do not mentally argue with the speaker. Do not create your grocery

---

14   Wayne W Dyer, Ph.D. *The Power of Intention.* Carlsbad, California: Hay House, Inc. 2004. Print.

list in your head, while appearing as though you are listening. Do not wait your turn to talk. Listen instead. There is so much to discover through active, engaged listening. Mine it for every insight that is available. Listen for the words that are used; the tone of the speaker's voice; the facial expression and body language (if present with the person); and, even listen for what is not said. There is great value to be had there.

Second, silence can be a useful tool for a coach leader. It offers the other person(s) the opportunity to consider, reflect, and then access their own insights and answers to options and challenges. Remember, depending on a person's communication style, time to think through something and create a response is very constructive. Listening presents us all with an opportunity to take style into account to become a more effective communicator.

2. **Tune In**

Engaged, clear listening requires that we not simply hear, but rather listen at a deeper level. In my own experience, observing hundreds of professionals and thousands of conversations in the workplace, I believe that many of us have, for a variety of reasons, developed a habit of superficial listening. We may think that we already know what the other person is going to say. We may have already decided on "the answer" and listening becomes nothing more than waiting our turn to manage or direct. Or we may be preoccupied and have not created the space to listen that we discussed above. As coaches, we are called on to tune in to our colleagues. Be interested rather than interesting. Suspend judgments; you really do not know what the other person is going to say. If you are physically present with the other person(s), face her; gently look her in the eyes. Invite the person to sit with you, if possible, with nothing separating you (sit on the same side of the desk or table). This does not mean that we need to invade someone's personal space. Allow the standard three to five feet between the two of you.

3. **Reflect Back**

From time to time in the course of a conversation, simply choose to let the other person know that you are engaged with them by telling them, in your own words, what you have heard so far. Do this when there is a natural lull in the conversation. Do not present your understanding as though it is fact. Simply present it as what you have heard so far and ask if you have it right. For example, "It sounds as though you...do I have that right?" Or, "Let me see if I'm hearing you correctly so far..." It is important to use your own words and not parrot back what the person just said.

4. **Constructively Label**

At times, as you reflect back what you have heard, it may be useful to offer a label for the feelings or thoughts that you are hearing. This is not done in a "know it all" way; rather, it is best offered as part of a question with the intention of helping the speaker to gain some insight and potentially take some action. For example, "It sounds to me from what you are describing that you feel really overwhelmed right now? Is that true?" If it is, then you can follow up by asking the person to identify one thing that they can do to feel just a little less overwhelmed. If not, then ask them to label their feelings more accurately.

5. **Clarify**

Sometimes, it is best to just admit that you aren't quite sure what the point is that the other person(s) is making. Something such as, "I'm not sure that I understand. Try to explain it in a different way so that I get it" can be helpful.

6. **Acknowledge**

Let the person know that you are fully engaged and tracking along with them in a conversation using either a verbal or non-verbal acknowledgement or prompt. The best known nonverbal prompt is a slight nodding of the head. A verbal prompt can also be useful and is the only way to get this job done when you are not physically with the other person. I often say, "Tell me more..." to encourage the speaker and let them know that I am engaged and interested. A simple *ummm humm* will do perfectly. Send consistent messages that you are really in the conversation with them, but don't overdo it.

7. **Summarize**

Finally, unless the conversation is a very short hallway exchange, it is critical to summarize your understanding of the outcome of your discussion. It continues to surprise me that four people leaving a business meeting can genuinely have four completely different understandings of the outcome. Take a minute or two to confirm your take on the conversation to be sure that your understanding is shared by the other person. A short written follow-up can also be helpful. Check in on your intention if you write a brief follow-up. Is it to be an effective communicator and contribute to a successful outcome? Or is it more about protecting yourself (CYA—covering your own a_ _)?

That's it. Seems small, doesn't it? Simple. Such changes can't possibly make a difference, right? Wrong. This is exactly what leading from your seat is all about. Taking the lead and changing your workplace one conversation, one relationship at a time. It can be really challenging to actively listen when you are rushed or the situation is charged and stressful. Start somewhere, anywhere today to develop a new listening habit and work your way up to difficult moments. Take action! Take the lead.

Coach Leader Behavior #2:
Intentional Languaging—Choose Words with Great Care

While engaged, clear listening is a powerful force in being a coach leader, it is one of *four* complementary elements of our coaching starter kit. In addition to great listening and positively exploiting knowledge of communication styles, intentional languaging is key to communicating effectively. Gently sharing what you hear in a caring and courageous way using the skills I'm about to introduce you to is what separates the good from the great in organizations.

I want to emphasize seven basic elements of intentional languaging. They are deceptively simple, but not easy to do day in and day out. As you master these, and they become habit instead of effort, you will take yet another step closer to being your best self at work and leading from your seat.

Choosing your words becomes even more powerful when coupled with active listening. Imagine, for a moment, that you are in a conversation with someone who is obviously and genuinely listening to your every word. There are no interruptions, no judgments, no subtle put downs. In fact, there are small signals that affirm and acknowledge you. Now imagine that, after listening intently to you, the other person in this conversation responds with well-chosen words that allow you to feel heard, while at the same time are clear and crisp, help you to dig deep for your own answers, and challenge your same-old, same-old way of thinking.

Honestly, how would you feel at the end of that imaginary conversation? If you are being honest, I think that you will conclude that you would feel pretty darn good. Stronger. More capable. Listened to. Heard. Relieved. Back on track.

That's the reward. And we get to co-create just those kinds of conversations at work. And, after you have found your coach leader groove, these conversations feel really good. It's a win. You do your part. Let others do theirs.

Seven Elements of Intentional Languaging

1. **Be crisp and clear**—Take the time to be crisp and clear in your communications. Be straightforward *without being harsh or blunt*. For many reasons, it seems to me that we have developed the opposite habit—we seem to work hard at intentional ambiguity! Think about it. We sacrifice clarity to avoid potential litigation; to sidestep conflict; to pretend that we know what we are talking about; to prove just how educated we are; or to try not to hurt someone else's feelings. We expect that others will read (or hear) between the lines and we cross our fingers that they will get our disguised messages. Finally, we become indignant when they don't get the message, even though we have not done our part by being clear.

   So, today begin to practice *clarity* by selecting the very best words for the situation and avoiding ambiguous words. Routinely begin to ask yourself: "Is this as clear as this message can be?" Also, avoid the use of superlatives unless they are essential for clarity. Every single situation cannot be a disaster! Routinely ask yourself for verification when you want to use a superlative: "Is it really true that he is NEVER on time?" "Does she ALWAYS yell when you ask a question?" There is a simple exercise at the end of the chapter to challenge you to *get clear* in your everyday conversations. Take the challenge!

2. **Apply the pronoun test**—Although they are some of the smallest words in our sentences, they send an important micro-message to the listener(s). Be intentional in their use. Use **"I"** when owning or describing your thoughts, feelings, perceptions, or opinions. Use **"we"** to share successes and team efforts and to emphasize partnerships, collaborations, and community. Be very aware of the tone of your voice when using the word "**you**."

   Of course, there is nothing wrong with the word "you" and it is frequently the clearest choice. Having said that, this word can land poorly with a blaming or accusatory tone of voice or a harsh choice of words. So, if you open up a conversation with something like, "I've been told that you're fighting with Mary, too!" you certainly aren't in the coaching space and it may feel as though you have reached a conclusion before hearing the listener's point of view. And adding the word "too" at the end would indicate that you think that this bad behavior is a pattern. An alternative might sound like, "I'm getting the sense that you and Mary disagree about the _____. Is that true? How did you two end up here? What is the plan to work through this?"

   Finally, who in the heck is **"they"**? When I ask team members who "they" are or "them" is when used in a sentence, the most frequent response is, you guessed it! "I don't know!" The second most frequent response is, "you know, them, the executives!" Remember our commitment to clarity. If everyone involved in a conversation is clear on who "they" is, then use it. Otherwise, choose a different, crisper way to describe those involved.

3. **Language the Positive**—I want to begin by telling you what this does *not* mean. Languaging the positive does not mean that we put on rose-colored glasses and ignore personal or organizational challenges. That's the workplace equivalent to rearranging the deck chairs on the Titanic. It also does not mean that we become a team of Pollyannas, sacrificing authenticity for over-the-top hyper-optimism. Now that we have that out of the way, we can talk about how profound an impact a constructive approach can have on an individual, a

team, or an entire organization. Great coach leaders know that there are plenty of opportunities to sincerely frame discussions in a positive or constructive way. They also realize the benefits that will almost immediately accrue to you and to those surrounding you when you choose to include positivity and possibility as part of your everyday leadership. Here is the short list of the benefits of routinely languaging the positive:

- ✓ Tap into innovation and creative problem solving more effectively.

- ✓ Predispose those around you to believe that things can "get right" and that they can play a role in making that happen.

- ✓ Reduce the time it typically takes to make mid-course corrections or manage/recover from a "crisis."

- ✓ Help to further establish a healthy workplace community.

- ✓ Engage in healthy, meaningful conflict.

- ✓ Learn more easily from challenges and failures.

- ✓ Set the stage to avoid making the same mistake in the future.

- ✓ Grow members of the team and unlock the best in everyone.

- ✓ Foster a safe environment in which accountability is consistently practiced.

Languaging the positive simply means that we choose the most positive and constructive words to fit the circumstances. In so doing, we become more effective communicators because, more often than not, we are getting our messages across in a way that the other person can hear them, let them in, and then do something with the information or knowledge. Yes, that's all there is to it! But remember, big doors swing on small hinges—little stuff makes a huge difference when done consistently.

There are some simple exercises to enhance your understanding of this concept at the end of the chapter. They focus on sentences and phrases that we could hear any day in a typical workplace. The challenge is to come off autopilot and really choose our words so that they are constructive. Give them a try on your own. Then use them to challenge your team.

4. **Describe Behavior Instead of Rushing to Judgment**—Some of my colleagues have shared with me that this element of intentional languaging—choosing to describe behavior rather than judge and label the behavior—is the most challenging new coaching skill to master and sustain. Why? I think that part of the explanation may be that we are all, in part, paid to and rewarded for making judgments! That's not a bad thing. But when it comes to behavior that is getting in someone's way, if we truly are committed to everyone's success, then we must use the most effective language to share our observations so that the person has the best chance of understanding and doing something about it.

It is *clearer* to describe a behavior than use a judgment that could well be misunderstood. For example, telling someone that they are not a "team player" is a vague judgment and it may be difficult for the person to know what to do differently to be a better team member. They may choose to feel misunderstood and resentful. These feelings, then, could give rise to other unproductive behaviors. If, on the other hand, we shared our observations by specifically describing a behavior (or an action) in a clear, charge neutral way, the other person has at least a better chance to get the picture we are portraying, have skillful discussion with us about it, and choose differently in the future. So, saying something like "Mary, in every team meeting for the past month, you have loudly disagreed with Steve on every point" gives the person a clear picture of what you have seen through your lens and what you have experienced. What happens next is engaged, clear listening and collaborative inquiry—otherwise known as coaching! Remember, you could be interpreting the situation incorrectly or you could be missing some key information. Talk before you pass judgment. Labels have an uncanny way of sticking with a person, even if they are inaccurate.

Don't miss the opportunity to practice this one! The exercises at the end of the chapter can be pretty tough.

5. **Practice civility, respect, and consideration**—In ALL interactions, regardless of the message or the choices that others make, we are called upon as coach leaders to be civil, respectful, and considerate. And to practice what I preach, I want to be clear about what I mean by "civil." According to Professor PM Forni, "civility is an attitude of thoughtfully relating to others. It means that we must first be aware of others and then weave restraint, respect, and consideration into the very fabric of that awareness."[15]

    This definition has a WOW-factor for me. I truly believe that if we all made civility a priority, we would be rewarded with a better world. While the subject of civility is a significant one for any coach leader, it is even more vital to the creation of workplace community, and for that reason merits a complete volume of its own in the *Everyday Leadership* Series. Look for it in the future. In practice, being civil, respectful, and considerate would mean that we do not engage in gossip in our organizations. It would require that we think the best of others until proven otherwise. Civility means that we don't interrupt someone. That we don't sacrifice the basics of "please and thank you" even when we are in a hurry. Most of us know, at some level, how to be civil. What we need to do now is to make it an everyday habit *again*!

6. **Tell the Story**—Storytelling is a right-brain activity. That makes it a strong match to the emerging organizational and leadership models that we learned about in Part 1. Many people in today's organizations want to know the details; they can handle the truth when it comes to financial data. But more than anything else, they want to be connected and inspired by a compelling story. Coach leaders understand this and make it their business to know how to communicate through story. They realize that the change process is better received and more easily sustained if everyone understands the story, the why behind

---

15   PM Forni. *Choosing Civility: The 25 Rules of Considerate Conduct.* New York: St. Martin's Griffin, 2003. Print.

the change. Although storytelling is more compatible with some communications styles, we all have the ability to add this to our communication repertoire. If this is not your current brilliance, check out some of the resources and suggestions in the Coaching TO GO section at the end of this chapter.

7. **Practice "What If" Upping**—Rounding out the seven elements of intentional languaging is a quirky but valuable skill. I don't know about you, but when I was growing up professionally, we paid an awful lot of attention to thinking about, talking about, preparing for, and strategizing around the "worst case scenario"! This isn't necessarily a bad thing. We should consider different possible outcomes and how we will respond. But I believe that we may have gone overboard in our emphasis of the worst possible outcome. If we are going to play this "what if" game, then I believe that we owe it to ourselves and our organizations to be balanced and play it both ways. How about spending thinking about, talking about, dreaming about, and strategizing about the "best case scenario"? I call that "what if" upping (as opposed to the traditional what ifs that seem to spiral ever downward).

As a coach leader, it is so important that you develop a habit of expecting the very best and navigating the flow. It is equally important for each of us to encourage and cultivate that in others around us. Remember, from our discussion of intentionality that thoughts become things, so choose the good ones. What we think about does indeed help to shape our next reality. The skillful communicator keeps this in mind as s/he makes idea and word selections. What if everyone in your organization began to focus their energy and attention on working toward a shared, positive vision of the future? What if that turned out to be pretty amazing? What if all it took to begin this trend was for one person to do it? What if that one person is you?

Being more conscious of your words and then making wise choices will help every single relationship or situation. It won't assure the outcome each time, but it will allow you to act as an adult, make a constructive contribution, control the things that you can, and become more influential. Intentional languaging can heal old wounds, be a time saver and help someone to feel better about herself. Some colleagues have asked if intentionally choosing your words isn't just being a little too PC (politically correct). Why can't we all just put on our big-girl and big-boy pants, they complain, and stop hanging on every word that is said.

I agree that we all must be adults and tell the truth as we see it. And we can all work on not taking every remark personally. Nevertheless, how we choose to message something will still be critically important to our level of success. Because this is about people, not machines. It is about creating community, not isolating one another. It is about engagement and that requires respect, consideration, and thoughtfulness. Intentional language is a huge WIN. It pays such big dividends once you get the rhythm of it. Make the effort. This is a terrific example of doing more than what is expected. You change you. And check out the results.

Coach Leader Behavior #3:
Intentional Nonverbal Messaging

When you and I are together (either co-located or via video conferencing), 93 percent of the message comes from something other than the words! What a huge opportunity to become a more effective communicator—take responsibility for and control of your facial expressions, postures, gestures, eye positions, tone of voice, and the sounds that you make (sometimes called para-linguals).

When it comes to nonverbal mastery, there are two things to keep in mind:

1. Align nonverbals with your words to maximize your effectiveness. When there is an inconsistency between the message that your words send and the message of your eyes or your body, most people will choose to "get the message" through the nonverbal communication channel. So, if someone responds to a request with the word "fine" and at the same time uses eyes, facial expressions, and postures to send a message of annoyance, the person receiving the message will most often

come away from the interaction believing that the person is annoyed.

Whenever I talk about nonverbals with an audience or within a specific organization, someone almost always shares with me that they genuinely don't know that they are—for example, rolling their eyes during the meeting. If you really do not know, then your body is doing things behind your back—does that make sense? I have come to understand that what most people mean is that those eye movements are not intentional; they are a habit that we do not think about. It feels as though we don't know but we are the only ones in charge of our body and we are the ones who developed the habit in the first place. And the good news is that we are the only ones who can make a new choice!

Be intentional. Send the most effective message that you can with your words coupled with your actions. If you feel annoyed, then own the feeling. Express it with civility and be prepared to discuss a solution with your boss or your teammate. This is the mature behavior of a coach leader.

2. The other consideration when it comes to nonverbals is to avoid becoming hyper-correct. Sometimes a scratch of the nose simply means that it is allergy season and someone has an itchy nose. What we need to focus on is noticing patterns in ourselves and others. If they add to effective communications then keep doing them—they are contributing to your coach leadership. If they aren't then we need to surrender them in favor of something better. Have some fun with the list of the most common nonverbal cues found in the workplace. It is included in the Coaching TO GO section of this chapter. Remember, don't over-read signs in yourself or others.

So there you have it, the three basic behaviors that are the heart and soul of coach leadership—the starter kit. These will set up you and your organization for successfully creating a new, broader appreciation for the value of personal accountability and embedding it as a cultural expectation.

But, we're not finished yet! When it comes to accountability, the coaching starter kit is primarily focused on helping each of us to be personally accountable more often and more visibly. The added bonus is that they also allow us to engage in more useful, more powerful conversations that have the potential to help others along their own trajectory toward uncompromising personal accountability.

That being said, there are two more, advanced behaviors that, when practiced and mastered, position each of us to be even more helpful to others and more influential culturally.

Advanced Coach Leader Behavior #1:
Collaborative Inquiry

Because coach leadership is about helping others to access their own solutions to problems and challenges and generate their own options when faced with opportunities or dilemmas, we need to become really good at asking questions. And those questions need to come from our heart and a true desire to work together or *collaborate.* This is very different for most of us. We are used to quickly, definitively, and assertively advocating for our opinion—or "telling" the other person what to do (or not do).

Collaborative inquiry is a core skill that sets coach leadership apart from traditional management approaches. It is almost like being an organizational Sherlock Holmes. In the spirit of bringing out the best in others, we ask deliberate (carefully chosen) and meaningful questions that will get people thinking and moving forward on their own.

As a coach leader, we give people just enough to solve their own problems, create their own solutions, and then get out of their way. Asking questions is also really good for the person doing the inquiring. It is a reminder to practice humility and to avoid the assumption that we always know best or have the whole picture.

Remember, for the collaborative inquiry process to yield the kind of results that we all want, we must activate our coach leader ear through engaged, clear listening and be intentional in our choice of words, gestures, postures, sounds, tone, etc. We must all avoid the temptation to simply advocate for our own ideas, at least right away. There often is a point in time to offer our insights, experiences, and suggestions. But it is best to allow the other person(s) ample time to come up with their own solutions. We have an active role to play in that process. Coach leaders are not by-standers or hand-holders. We can make a vital contribution by asking relevant, high-quality questions—the more specific and intentional the question the better.

The initial step to mastering collaborative inquiry is to simply make it your habit to ask more questions. There are several different types of questions and all of them have a meaningful place in the collaborative inquiry process:

✪ Background Questions—These can introduce a topic, get the story behind a situation, and/or allow you to understand the context.

> Example: What is the medical history of this patient?

✪ Open-ended Questions—These invite others to explain, describe, explore, and/or elaborate.

> Example: Can you describe the problem with your computer?

✪ Close-ended Questions—These narrow the discussion to specific information.

> Example: What is the cost of this education program?

✪ Confirming Questions—These clarify understanding.

> Example: So, if your computer is upgraded this afternoon, you can complete the monthly census report by the end of the day on Friday?

✪ Coaching or Probing Questions—These go deeper into a situation or an issue. They have a coaching purpose. They are very intentional. They are the portal through which our colleagues can begin to develop their own solutions. We will discuss these in detail below as they are the backbone of collaborative inquiry and the coaching model itself. But I want you to consider this: because the questions of a coach leader are so specific and so intentional, they have spontaneity to them. They arise from what happens in a conversational moment with other people. Generic examples often don't do them justice.

I want to share with you what I consider to be one of the simplest, yet most powerful, questions that a coach leader can begin to use regularly. Ready? Here it is: "What do you think?" Followed by silence. Think about this elegant question. You are sending an important series of messages to the other person by using this question. It says, "You're smart and I value your opinion." It says, "I expect that you are thinking about this and have a solution to offer." It says, "You're a leader." Tom Peters provocatively states that these four words are the most important four words in business environments. And for me, it is *no* accident that they come in the form of a question.

Developing a habit of asking questions instead of giving into the temptation of telling, directing, avoiding, or even lobbying for our preferred solution is a **huge** first step. Concentrate on this discipline. It is important to acknowledge that, especially at first, it will take more time to ask questions and engage in collaborative inquiry. Being "charge neutral" or non-judgmental when asking questions is critically important. Consider these examples:

> **Charge Neutral Question**: "What was your intention behind the email to Robert?"
> **Judgmental Question**: "Why did you stir the pot and send Robert that provocative email?"
> **Charge Neutral Question**: "What's the timeline that you typically follow for releasing meeting minutes?"
> **Judgmental Question**: "Why are *you always* so late in getting out our meeting minutes?"

Sometimes, we convince ourselves that in the interest of time, we will take a short cut—just this once—and just tell someone what to do. And truly, there are legitimate circumstances when we *need to be* directive. But those times are exceptions. Remember, this is about "teaching a person to fish." Slow down to speed up.

Collaborative Inquiry is such a rich, powerful segment of our learning and is absolutely essential to the coach leader model and to **full-throttle engagement** that it deserves a summary. Here goes:

Coach leaders intentionally replace the habit of "telling people around us what to do" with the new habit of asking questions of others. This is immensely beneficial because it allows the other person to create their own solutions, to take moderate risks, to become more effective decision makers, and to more fully engage in the everyday life of the organization. Coaching questions are complemented by coaching observations and requests. They share the following characteristics:

- ✪ They always have a purpose beyond simply gathering information. They assist the other person and make a contribution to forward momentum.

- ✪ They often interrupt typical thought patterns—in other words, they can help people to free themselves from a "thought rut."

- ✪ They sometimes result in instant illumination—a "V8 moment" or a "blinding flash of the obvious."

- ✪ They genuinely have the potential to result in breakthroughs.

- ✪ They must flow from engaged, clear listening, especially tuning in fully to the other person, and intentional nonverbal messaging.

- ✪ They are always offered in a spirit of non-judgmentalism. They are not manipulative.

- ✪ They stem from connecting head, heart, and gut. They must be genuine and specific.

Advanced Coach Leader Behavior #2:
Building Others

One of the most compelling reasons to use the coach leader model and one of its most valuable benefits is that the model calls on each of us to not only uncover the best in ourselves, but also to help those around us—including our boss, our colleagues, those who may report to us, and those that we encounter throughout our work day—to discover and embrace their best selves as well.

Once this virtuous cycle gets rolling in an organization, it feeds itself! I focus on your greatness and help you to see yourself through my eyes. You, in turn, are uplifted by the experience and mirror the experience back to me. This building behavior can become infectious and as it spreads, the cycle repeats itself. There comes a point when the energy of the organization changes to match the constructive energy of the building process. Then, the team as a whole is on a roll and becomes an amazing point of attraction for goodness and possibility. Now that's full-throttle engagement. I have had the professional opportunity to be a part of such an organization. And I have watched it unfold in other organizations as a coach. It was magical. I want each of you to have that same experience.

Can you also connect a few more dots and see how this virtuous cycle can set a team or an organization on course for increasing levels of accountability? That engagement and accountability go hand in glove? That coaching is the energy conductor for both?

In my coaching opinion, which has been shaped by hundreds of coaching observations and coaching conversations, one of the most interesting aspects of recognizing greatness in others and helping them to claim their best selves is that it is ***impossible to authentically recognize the greatness in another unless and until we acknowledge the greatness within ourselves.***

If you have not spent the time identifying, celebrating, and then cultivating your own greatness, you run the risk of missing the mark when highlighting the greatness in others. Your coaching comments may land on the other person as hollow or insincere. Remember, from our earlier conversations—you must begin working on yourself first. Coach yourself to greatness. Only then can you effectively help another(s). Revisit the chapters on the Coach Leader Model and Intentionality if you need to refresh and recommit.

I know that I am stating what is painfully obvious to most of us but it needs to be said—many of us show up to the workplace with defeating self-talk, lingering self-doubts, and a relatively limited view of who we are and what is possible. I am confident that as you have practiced intentionality more and more in your life and managed your thoughts, feelings, beliefs, and behaviors, that you have shed most of those same-old, same-old habits. But many of those around us each day have not yet started that work and are still stuck in a downward spiral. Remember, thoughts become things! It is true even if the thoughts are negative.

As you choose to build others around you, you will begin to notice that you more naturally see the brilliance in others. And want the best for them. I often hear, "I can't believe that I didn't see that in him before." Once you get the hang of this skill you will be amazed at how rewarding it is! It feels good and it is heartwarming to help someone else to turn on to and tap into their signature strengths! Often, we begin to see someone else's next level of achievement or their real potential before they do.

When we communicate clearly and authentically the vision that we have of others, we help them to capture that vision for themselves and believe more boldly in who they are and who they can become in the future. Building another simply means that we help others to, first, become aware of their positive attributes and then, use those attributes more and more frequently in thought, word and behavior in the workplace.

Building others is not one skill, but rather a constellation of mini (small but mighty) skills woven together to create powerful change. These mini skills are described below. They rely completely on action. Clear listening and collaborative inquiry. The **Coaching TO GO** section contains exercises and suggestions for growing and sustaining these skills within yourself.

Mini Skills:

Assisting Others in Recognizing their Own Greatness—Many of my colleagues tell me that it is much easier to focus on the negative—or what is wrong with them—than appreciating their brilliances and uniqueness and celebrating their accomplishments at work and elsewhere. Our self-talk can be defeating and limiting. This often gets in the way of both our ability to craft a compelling vision for our future and our ability to move ahead and be our best selves. In other words, we can get caught in this downward spiraling conversation within ourselves. It's tough to break free from such a place.

As a coach leader, we have the privilege of helping others to claim the best that is in them. I affectionately call this "feed forward" (as opposed to feedback) because it can be so helpful in propelling us ahead!

Gradually, as we consistently hold up a mirror for the other person and as we choose to focus on their strengths, their own downward spiraling conversations will begin to recover and spiral up instead. Often, our colleagues feel a surge of energy as confidence increases and self- doubts decrease.

The way forward is a bit easier as old negative roadblocks are removed. Those around us may enjoy one or more of the following benefits as a direct result of our willingness to consistently see the best in them and our help in allowing them to see it as well:

- A new, more positive sense of self (a look in the mirror)
- New self-talk to match a new self-awareness
- More available energy
- More clarity and excitement about future opportunity
- Growing self confidence

To allow others to see themselves in a positive light as an individual with amazing potential, we must start with laying a sturdy foundation upon which they can build themselves. That means that through engaged, clear listening; intentional languaging; powerful questioning; and truth telling, we can:

- Allow them to better understand who and where they are today and who and where they want to be in the future. This may mean that they consider what gives them satisfaction, how they define their own personal happiness, and what they identify as their source of passion. Being a coach leader is all about working in the critical gap—helping another to move from where they are today to where they want to be in the future.

- Remind someone that where they are today is "perfect enough," one part of their overall journey toward becoming her/his best self.

- Co-create with others possible ways to play to their brilliances and to leverage their strengths in the workplace.

When building another through coach leadership, we must be ever mindful of one of coaching's fundamental principles: it is a brilliance-based or strength-based leadership approach. We are called upon to spend the majority (80 percent) of our time, energy, and attention focused on **strengths,** our own and others.

---

*The greatest good you can do for another is not just
To share your riches, but to reveal to him his own.*

Benjamin Disraeli

Building another also gives us the perfect opportunity to celebrate "the incomplete leader." In place of command and control, today's everyday leaders must be able to cultivate and coordinate the actions of others throughout the organization. They need to embrace the ways in which they are incomplete in order to be able to fill in their knowledge gaps with others' skills. Incomplete leaders differ from incompetent leaders in their ability to recognize their own growing edges (others refer to these as weaknesses) as well as strengths, and in having the confidence and humility to recognize unique talents and perspectives throughout the organization.

Deborah Ancona, in her article titled "In Praise of the Incomplete Leader," declares that "it's time to end the myth of the complete leader... Expecting leaders to do everything right, to be perfect, to be *complete*. No leader is perfect. The best ones don't try to be. They concentrate on honing their strengths and find others who can make up for their limitations."[16] This is what building others is all about. It creates leaders in every seat in the organization. Through it we create an interdependent web in the workplace that harmonizes strong business results with meaning and satisfaction.

Now what? What can I do with my new understanding of helping others to recognize their own brilliance that will make a difference at work and help me to lead from my seat?

Do what Carol did. She is the COO of a successful ambulance company in the southeastern U.S. She masterfully turned around the financial picture for the company in less than eighteen months. And she was a wiz at creating policies and procedures to tighten up operations. However, when it came to building key relationships with hospitals and nursing homes in their service area, she was out of her comfort zone.

It was hard to accept that she wasn't all that good at connecting with people. She intentionally chose to see this as an opportunity to allow another person in the organization to really shine and grow. She arranged a lunch with Devon, the Director of Marketing. She had come to admire the ease with which he developed relationships and his good stewardship of them once they were in place. She asked him to be her partner in forging new alliances in the market place. He eagerly agreed and he took the lead with a passion. She

---

16   Deborah Ancona, Thomas W Malone, Wanda J Orlinski and Peter Senge. "In Praise of the Incomplete Leader," *Harvard Business Review*, February 2007. Pages 110-117. Print.

learned a great deal from working with Devon. She developed relationships too. But she continued to recognize Devon's contribution and encouraged him to do more. Devon independently developed an in-house course on building great relationships, which he proudly delivered himself many times.

Several years later, Devon left the company to take on a more senior position with an international marketing firm. Building this young leader, making room for his seat at the leadership table, and practicing humility helped everyone involved. This is also an example of the power of followership.

What's right questioning? In the previous coach-leader behavior on collaborative inquiry, I talked about a framework for asking questions that accentuates the positive. The "what's right" questioning framework can also be a useful ally when it comes to assisting others in unleashing their best selves at work. Think about it. What better way to initiate or expand a conversation on someone's greatness than by reviewing all of the things that are working or going well in that person's experience? Conversely, when something is not going well, one of the most powerful ways to turn the situation around is to ask "what's right" as opposed to finding fault and making everyone and everything wrong.

Because "what's right" questions are so instrumental in successful coach leadership, I am repeating them here to refresh your memory:

What are all of the things that are working?

How did this happen?

What's not right yet?

How can we make things even better?

At times our own light goes out and
Is rekindled by a spark from another person.
Each of us has cause to think with deep gratitude
Of those who have lighted the flame within us.

Albert Schweitzer

Affirming and Communicating Belief—As you may have noticed by now, the mini skills of building another person are very, very simple. In fact, they are deceptively simple. They might seem too small or even insignificant to make a difference in our relationships with others. And we might dismiss them out of turn. That would be unfortunate.

While these mini skills are simple, they can have a major impact on someone else. This is the case with affirming and then sharing your belief in someone else. Knowing that you believe that someone is special in their work life and that you have confidence in their abilities and in who they are can give that person the turbo charge that they need to surge forward. Or it just might provide that one extra ounce of confidence that they need to reach a milestone or overcome an obstacle that has haunted them for some time.

Right about now, some of you may be thinking "my colleagues know that I believe in them…I don't need to say it out loud." Others have told me that it sounds corny or condescending to tell someone that you believe in them. "I can't say that to my boss or to my peer!" As a coach who has spent a great deal of time *listening* in many different types of organizations, I can tell you that these are not my truths. People around us need to hear regularly that we believe in them. It never gets old if offered sincerely. They stand just a bit straighter. They do just a bit more. They take a larger risk. They play bigger.

This example demonstrates just how simple this behavior can be in interactions. *Your colleague at work has just been promoted to a very visible, very prestigious position. Initially, she was filled with confidence. After two months of challenges, however, she is increasingly filled with doubts and fear that she cannot be effective in the job. You are 100 percent certain that she can do the job and more. The simple gift of telling her that—specifically and emphatically—could be the turning point for her to gain traction and move forward.*

Sorting the past/present/future—The final mini skill to building someone is to assist them in properly sorting the past from the present and the future. Many times, the best of us can get stuck thinking that the past necessarily predicts the future. It doesn't, by the way. We can change. We can choose a different behavior. We can grow a different habit.

As a coach leader in our organization we can help others by reminding them that *our point of power is in the present moment.* We cannot change the past but we can definitely learn from what happened. One of my favorite quotes from Mother Theresa was a response that she gave when criticized for changing her position on some issue. She simply said, "I didn't know then what I know now." How simple. How elegant.

Similarly, through intentionality, we become architects of our own future. How we choose to think, feel, and act in the present will, in large measure, shape our future. That means that we are in the driver's seat when it comes to our own experience. Helping others to see this and to act from this knowledge will allow them to reclaim their own personal power and make strides to being at their best at work.

Coach Leadership Inventory

At its core, coaching is a potent, purposeful way of communicating that helps others grow and enhance their own effectiveness and feel supported in the process. This is so easy to discount and yet so very important for each and every one of us to understand and act upon.

Coach leadership is a relationship—a success partnership!! Bottom line, then, is that we must relentlessly stretch ourselves to be extra-ordinary communicators. That's our super power! To make every word, every facial expression, every interaction count. We need to understand and then develop a sophisticated skill set in order to meet this challenge.

To top off our skinny review of the coaching behaviors that are most relevant when creating a culture of owners, I've also included a brief coach leader inventory as a learning tool. Remember, EVERYONE coaches—up, down and across in our organization! For those of you who are actively working on building these skills, the inventory will act as a refresher and a self-assessment. For others, the statements themselves emphasize the critical skills of the coach leader model and provide perspective on your current mastery level.

The Inventory

Directions: For each statement, select a response that best describes the degree to which it is characteristic of your everyday behaviors/approach at work. Consider all of your daily interactions when making your choice—with your boss, peers and team members throughout your organization. Please provide an answer to all of the statements using the following scale:

1= Rarely 2 = Sometimes 3 = Many times 4 = Most Times 5 = Almost Always

Definitions

Rarely—Almost never. Ten percent or less of the time
Sometimes—Over 10 percent up to half or 50 percent of the time
Many times—Over 50 percent to 75 percent of the time
Most times—Frequently. 75 percent to 90 percent of the time
Almost Always—Over 90 percent of the time.

The Coaching Framework	Rating
I see myself as others' success partner.	
I treat others as capable, well-intended adults	
I willingly consider others' ideas and solutions.	
I choose to think the best of others.	
I actively help others to learn & grow; to be the best version of themselves.	
I successfully resist the temptation to fix people or their problems.	
I do my part to co-create a safe, supportive environment.	
I encourage others to identify their own solutions.	
I ask others' questions rather than tell them what to do	
The Basic Behaviors of a Coach Leader	**Rating**
I listen clearly and actively when someone is talking to me.	
I use silence as a coaching tool.	
I avoid interrupting others or finishing their sentences.	
I paraphrase what someone has said to be sure that I understand them correctly.	
I avoid multi-tasking when I listen.	
I choose my words with great care so that my message is clear.	
I deliver my message as positively & constructively as the situation permits.	
I practice civility, respect and consideration in my interactions.	
I intentionally choose my non-verbal messages.	
I give feedback that describes behavior rather than making vague judgements or personal attacks.	

Advanced Behaviors of a Coach Leader	Rating
I ask powerful, thought-provoking questions to help others grow.	
I challenge others by making powerful requests & observations.	
I share my perceptions (my truth) in a way that others can hear.	
I focus most on what's right or what's working.	
I let others know that I believe in them.	
I know the signature strengths (brilliances) of others.	
I encourage others to stretch beyond comfortable inaction to new performance levels.	
I help others to set and achieve big goals.	
I use fun and play as important leadership approaches.	

Now, by design there is no "score" associated with this inventory. I don't want you to be too hooked into using a score to determine if you are a coach leader. Rather, I prefer to think of that development process as a never-ending evolution. We don't ever get this work done! There's always something to refine and we're always re-setting the bar on what's good and what's great. So, as an additional **leadership challenge**, why not

- ✪ Circle one item on which you'll choose to focus for the next month (and then another one the following month and so on...)

- ✪ Plan on taking this inventory in, say, three months. Think of it as a tune-up similar to your car's regular maintenance.

8

The Unlearning: Recognizing and Changing Habits That Short Circuit Accountability

---

"The illiterate of the 21st century will not be those who cannot read and write but those who cannot learn, unlearn, and relearn."

Alvin Toffler

The very first action any organization needs to take, once it's adopted the coach-leader system of "directed conversation with oneself and with others that is aimed at helping, growing, and challenging" all team members to grow towards a more accountable enjoyable, and rewarding workplace, is to apply it to help one another to unlearn outdated or unhelpful habits.

As a leadership coach, I talk about the importance of unlearning all the time! I can make a strong business case for seeing it as equally, if not more important than the learning process. And I'm a huge fan of life-long learning, so you know the value that I place on a person's willingness and ability to confront current habits of thought, emotion, belief and behavior and then let go of those that are misfits or obstacles to top performance

Nowhere is this truer than the practice of personal accountability. For many of us, living the Accountability Credo day in and day out demands that we examine long held beliefs and actions and make sustainable, permanent changes. I think that Alvin Toffler nailed it in his quote (printed above).

We commit to the virtuous change cycle of learning—unlearning—and relearning.

Here's what Toffler's words mean to me:

Learning—Taking a fresh look at our everyday interactions and responsibilities for ways to role model personal accountability. Scouring leadership and industry specific educational materials for hints on new tips, tools, techniques, mindsets and practices. Observing and adopting others' best accountability practices.

Unlearning—Challenging our current assumptions, expectations and behavioral choices and discarding old habits or outdated responses from our memory. This is tough because you're letting go of things that may have helped you to be successful (or get along) in the past; or habits that have been a part of you for so long that they feel "true" or "right" or justified by the situation.

Relearning—Just as water can be frozen, thawed and then refrozen into an entirely different shape, so it is with our habits. Relearning completes the cycle by allowing us to embed new habits and practices as replacements for the old. We become better and different.

Remember this picture? It's my version of the stone wall that stands between us and a workplace culture of owners who unfailingly practice personal accountability (from page 32). Each stone in the wall represents an "unlearning" opportunity and now it's time to deconstruct that wall and clear the path ahead. Grab your leadership pick and shovel and let's get to it.

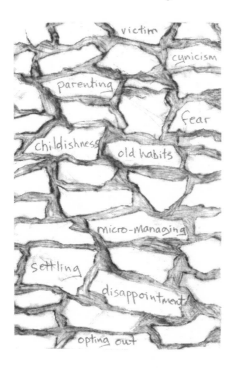

These are *the ten most unwanted* individual and organizational habits that prevent us from firmly establishing and growing an accountability-rich culture.

Accountability's Ten Most Unwanted List

Unlearn...

...that accountability rests only with *the leaders* who are only found at the top of the organization. That old traditional *vertical hierarchy* no longer works. It's on life support. It's futile to get better at a model that gets wronger with every passing day. It's being replaced with *horizontal hierarchy* in which everyone is expected to lead from their seats. Therefore, you are a leader. You have a daily responsibility to show up and do the right thing in each interaction and every task.

...that playing the role of a parent is an acceptable substitute for leadership. We are all adults at work. Protecting, enabling, nagging, punishing, hovering over and/or guilt tripping your colleagues are habits that have no legitimate place at work. They subtly (and maybe not so subtly) reinforce the message that others aren't capable of holding themselves accountable. Instead use powerful communication and coaching skills to share the fresh leadership expectations rooted in the Accountability Credo and universally apply them to everyone.

...that acting like a child is the best response to a parenting dynamic. Grow up already! Regardless of generation, stop trying to "get away with" stuff you know is not right, ignoring or defying policies or procedures, throwing temper tantrums or having melt downs. Do nothing that encourages someone else's parenting habit. The same goes for the middle school behaviors of cheating, gossiping, name-calling, being mean and creating cliques. They weren't right back in the day and they definitely aren't you at your best at work.

...cynicism. Is it just me or is cynicism on the rise? It shows up either as broad distrust of others and their motives and the organization in general or a deep, dark skepticism and negativity. If I thought for one minute that it would fire people up and spark action, I might feel differently about it. But my observations tell me that rarely happens; instead, it leads to blame-storming, conversations of disappointment and active disengagement. In fact, some have convinced themselves that they are entitled to their cynicism as the only "real" response to today's issues. At the heart of cynicism is a world view that someone else is always responsible. And it's someone else's job to fix what's broken. If the cynic accepts any personal accountability, it is very narrowly focused. It's a potent brand of toxin and if we don't take swift action to counter its effects, it will hold an organization hostage.

...the victim mentality. Often described as the "poor me" attitude, individuals see themselves as powerless in their environment. As someone once said to me, "I'm like a cork bobbing on the ocean, at the mercy of the tides..." The language used by victims is a pretty clear indicator of this mental model. As is the case with the cynic, victims seem almost allergic to personal accountability. If you see yourself as having no power or control, then you can't be accountable. My truth is that you do have power and influence, perhaps far more than you think. And you do have everyday choices. Your work does matter.

...that *settling* is okay. No, I don't mean to resolve (or settle) a dispute. Instead, I'm referring to the adult choice of a lower standard of conduct or performance. Settling for average or the way things are today rather than shooting for great, exceeding expectations and doing what's right.

...conversations consumed by disappointment. When the language in an organization is dominated by references to disappointment, it's a telltale sign that accountability is *not* an embedded cultural habit. Team leaders are sooo disappointed in their team members' responses; staff is soo discouraged that their department leader isn't fixing things fast enough; we express regular disappointment that our team mates get more favorable schedules, do less work, get away with _____ or that we aren't valued enough for our contributions; and little that the organization does seems right enough. Occasionally, we're going to experience disappointment; it's only human. But, when it's the dominant sentiment, we've derailed and need a midcourse correction! At the heart of a preoccupation with disappointment is a sense that someone else is responsible or to blame. That accountability rests with someone or something other than you.

...dysfunctional comfort. Each of us is personally accountable for being the best version of ourselves each day. When we perform on autopilot, we put our habits in the driver's seat. We do things because we've done them before, not because they're the right thing to do in the moment. Being familiar is not the same as being right. If you want more on dysfunctional comfort, re-read Chapter 4 in *Take The Lead*.

...the practice of "opting out." We don't get to decide which rules, processes, practices and procedures we're going to follow. Or which expectations do or do not apply to us. This disengagement is so prevalent that we have clever names for it: Retired while on active duty. Dead worker walking. When you hear, "I'm only here to collect a paycheck" you can bet that person is disengaged. The same is true when you see someone do the absolute minimum (over and over again) to avoid dismissal.

...fear. I'll admit that holding oneself accountable requires courage at times. It may not always be a popular response. Some of us may have had bad experiences in the past when we did the right thing and it did not turn out as we had expected. We're reluctant to do it again. Once bitten, twice shy. Well, the past doesn't necessarily predict the future. And just because it's scary, doesn't make it less right.

***

If we want to bring down the wall that separates us from a culture of accountability then we first must let go of any sense that we are entitled to any of these habits. You can't be an adult doing the right thing and hang on to them. These habits and the Accountability Credo are mutually exclusive.

We need to make shift happen!

SHIFT...

FROM	TO
Vertical hierarchy; leaders only at the top of the pyramid	Horizontal hierarchy; everyone leads from their seats
Parenting	Teaming; collaborating
Acting as a child	Showing up as a capable adult
Cynicism	Realistic optimism; being trusting and trustworthy
Victim	Powerful chooser
Settling for average	Being the best version of you
Conversations of disappointment	Conversations of action and possibility
Dysfunctional comfort	Intentional choice
Opting out	Full throttle engagement
Fear	Courage; hope

Identifying the shift is the easy part. Now to break the grip of these toxic habits, we must align new thoughts with new behaviors to produce better and different experiences, to be accountable as individuals and as an organizational culture.

Clearing up our habits will require the ongoing application of an antidote. For that, we need to access our coaching toolbox. You'll find everything you'll need there. If your skills are rusty or stale, it's time to refresh and recommit.

Re-read relevant sections of *Take The Lead,* Volume 1 of this Everyday Leadership Series and create some new goals and action items. Use the following hints to focus your work.

Toxic Habit	Antidote
Limiting belief that leaders are only at the top of a vertical hierarchy and they alone are accountable for the success of the organization.	Challenge your thinking through intentionality daily. Practice followership more by allowing others to take the lead. Delegate more and more effectively. Use words to encourage leadership at all levels. Never use the word "subordinate" again! Create adult relationships with your teammates.
Parenting others around you.	Regardless of generational differences, reinforce the framework that we are all adult colleagues who have contributions to make. Never refer to yourself as mom or dad, even as a joke. Never refer to your team as "the kids." Practice transparent communication to avoid protecting others from reality. Avoid nagging, micro-managing, excessive cheerleading and punishing behavior.
Choosing childish behaviors/responses.	Do the really tough work of being self-aware and recognizing these behaviors for what they are. Replace them with good will, generosity, a default position of thinking the best of others and a wholehearted commitment to doing the right thing. You are always in charge of your own choices. Choose to be a capable adult regardless of others' behaviors. Use words that convey that message.

Toxic Habit	Antidote
Responding cynically	Take steps to restore trust with others. Beware selective perception. Listen to others' perspectives without dismissal. Be slow to judge others as wrong. Fiercely question your own thinking. Ask yourself, "Is that really true?" Skip the sarcastic remarks. Be mindful of your non-verbal cues. Confront cynicism in others through crisp, straightforward coaching conversations about expectations and consequences. Apply consequences fearlessly. Acknowledge and reinforce constructive adult choices when they happen. Limit the impact of cynics on others through transparency, role modeling and trust building.
Playing the role of a victim	Start to reclaim your power in small ways. Focus on your circle of influence and exercise control where/when you can. Shift into problem solving mode. Offer a solution/option. Take small risks. Focus on helping others instead of fretting about yourself. Watch your words! Use strong words to describe yourself. List your signature strengths. At the end of each day, list three ways in which you were memorable in a good way.
Settling for being average	Build and grow yourself. Believe in yourself. Highlight times from the past when you did something great. Inspire yourself by noticing the greatness in others. Choose your company carefully; hang out with winners! Ask for coaching. Identify a mentor.

Toxic Habit	Antidote
Expressing disappointment globally and regularly	Choose your words and comments with care. Avoid using the word disappointment for a day. Then another…
Tolerating dysfunctional comfort	Question everything that you do. Ask yourself if it's a best practice; if it's not, then do something different. Confront your own personal brand of inertia that's holding you back and keeping you stuck. Ask others for feedback on your willingness to change and grow. Identify a success partner and task him/her to cue you when you resist new ideas or approaches.
Opting Out	Create your very own "commitment statement." Review your organization's standards of behavior as well as your team's rules of engagements. Recommit yourself to both by signing your name to each. Skip the excuses and justifications. They're all bogus. At the end of each day, notice all of the instances in which you honored your commitment and held yourself accountable.
Acting from fear	Fear comes from a primitive part of your brain. And it's not entirely a bad thing; it warns us of real danger. But there are times when it's hyper-vigilant and sends you the wrong signals. Your job is to make sure that you're accessing your whole brain when evaluating a threat. Coach yourself through it. Use your self-talk to confront everyday fears and affirm accountable behavior. Don't believe in your fears; connect instead to your core strength.

Accountability TO GO

Now, it's your turn to bring down the stone wall that's keeping you from leading a fully accountable lifestyle at work. Take the coaching challenge:

Identify one to three items of accountability's ten most toxic habits or behaviors that if shifted, would make the biggest positive impact for you. In one sentence, describe where you are today; do the same for where you want to be in one hundred days. Then, for each toxic habit or behavior, commit to three specific actions (antidotes). Consider this your mini accountability plan! If you're determined and persistent, in just one hundred days, you will have unlearned the old and relearned the new and you'll be on your way to **Owning It**!

....

Toxic Habit/Behavior #1:

——

Where am I today?

_____

_____

_____

_____

Where will I be in 100 days?

_____

_____

_____

_____

What specific actions will I take to get there?

_____

_____

_____

_____

Toxic Habit/Behavior #2:

_____

Where am I today?

_____

_____

_____

Where will I be in 100 days?

_____

_____

_____

_____

What specific actions will I take to get there?

_____

_____

_____

_____

Toxic Habit/Behavior #3:

_____

Where am I today?

_____

_____

_____

Where will I be in 100 days?

_____

_____

_____

What specific actions will I take to get there?

_____

_____

_____

_____

_____

_____

_____

9

Performance Matters: Behaving Our Way to Higher Levels of Accountability

---

"You can't talk your way out of that which you behaved yourself into; you must behave your way out."

Soulvolutional Way Poster

Paraphrasing Stephen Covey

We've already covered such jugular topics in Part Three that they merit a quick summary before we push on together.

First, a quick review of the definition of accountability:

Personal Workplace Accountability is accepting the responsibility to do the right thing consistently day in and day out in both tasks and relationships to live the Mission and Values of the organization and advance its Vision.

To create an accountability-rich workplace where people are doing the *right thing most of the time* takes some time, practice, and attention.

To accomplish that requires the specific work I have covered here in this section:

In Chapter Six, we painted a crisp, clear picture of the look and feel of a culture of accountability. I highlighted the powerful accountability mantra—*What You Permit, You Promote* and emphasized the chain of accountability. Finally, I offered two simple inventory tools to encourage thoughtful consideration of the choices that we make every day.

Chapter Seven offered a skinny review of the coach leader approach to workplace relationships. It emphasized the need for each of us to show up as the very best version of ourselves using the language, skills, framework and assumptions of coaching's rich tradition. While there are other workable options, coach leadership is the best fit when it comes to optimally using the Accountability Compass. This chapter covered both the skills included in the Coaching Starter Kit as well as two particularly consequential advanced skills, that, when aimed intentionally give us the power to act as accountable adults and position us ideally to help others do the same.

In Chapter Eight, the Un-learning, we unveiled Accountability's Ten Most Unwanted List and discussed individual and organizational habits that prevent us from building and growing a culture of accountability. And, as a bonus, we shared the coaching secrets that will unhook us from these debilitating habits for good!

The stage is now set for us to drill down to a more granular level on common organizational behaviors that either lift us up as accountable adults or keep us down in a low performance orbit.

As leaders from our seats, we must be quick to recognize the good, the bad and the ugly in our own behavior, the behaviors of our team mates and behaviors across the entire organization. Because, we are individually accountable to do all that we can to assure success at all three of those tiers.

Accountability Performance Zones

Accountability Performance Zones offer a way to sort everyday micro-behaviors that exemplify accountability from those that erode it. Here are just a few of the ways that they can give us a strategic advantage:

They yield a self-coaching snapshot of where we are today and, potentially, what behaviors we need to embrace to grow as leaders.

They help us to do a better job of coaching others around us, including our peers and our boss so that they can quickly identify blind spots and step up to higher levels of accountability.

They help us to more easily observe significant jumps in accountability (up or down).

They open the door for crucial conversations across the organization.

And they can be a valuable resource for those of us who participate in others' performance evaluations and provide more formal feedback.

Now, there might be a raised eyebrow or two out there about the use of Performance Zones. After all, an attendee at one of my recent speaking engagements accurately pointed out, "I thought that, for coach leaders, it was better to talk about the specific behavior rather than *label* someone. Unfavorable labels have a way of outliving the behavior to which they originally referred." It's a fair point!

What it comes down to is our intent in using them. Mine is constructive rather than destructive. And, as you can see, from the advantages listed above, they help me to be the best coach that I can be—for myself and for all others. When I see a pattern of behaviors, I see in which Zone it fits best. That cues me to a set of coaching skills, techniques and approaches that would be most useful. You'll still want to tailor any conversation to the individual involved but the Zone aims you in a more targeted direction.

Accountability Performance Zones roughly align with the well-known stoplight approach for categorizing everyday behaviors.

Green indicates healthy, helpful behaviors that demonstrate high levels of personal accountability.

Yellow identifies an average pattern of accountability habits or inconsistent behavioral choices.

Red includes behavioral habits that run counter to a pattern of accountability.

Let's dive deeper and take a more detailed look at the behaviors associated with each Performance Zone. As you absorb these descriptions...

1. **First, ask yourself from what Zone you operate most often. Where do you fit best?**
2. **Then, think of other team members or colleagues; what behaviors do they regularly choose? From your experience with them, in which Zone do they perform most often?**
3. **Finally, capture your insights in the space provided.**

Green Zone—The Accountability Role Model represents, on average, 15 percent of team members across organizations. That metric rises as more emphasis is placed on co-creating a culture punctuated by firmly held expectations of full adult accountability.

- ✪ Arrives at work early and stays until the day's work is done; rarely absent and only for legitimate reasons
- ✪ Is constructive & positive
- ✪ Is a creative solution seeker
- ✪ Often thought of as a "go to" person
- ✪ Is a great, steady influence on others
- ✪ Is an excellent steward of relationships; trustworthy
- ✪ Exceeds expectations
- ✪ Follows all everyday policies such as taking breaks, making personal phone calls, leaving work area (even when no one is watching)
- ✪ Delivers predictably high quality work, regardless of assignment
- ✪ Demonstrates strong commitment to making things better for the team and organization
- ✪ Consistently communicates respectfully & effectively. No we/they talk. No gossip. No back-biting.
- ✪ Is willing to help/coach others
- ✪ Provides frequent feedback; seeks and accepts constructive feedback
- ✪ Is eager to learn & improve
- ✪ Asks for more challenges or responsibility
- ✪ Anticipates needs or next steps; sees more of the big picture

Yellow Zone—The Accountability Student is the largest Zone; it includes approximately 65 – 70 percent of team members.

- ★ Demonstrates good attendance; usually arrives and leaves on time
- ★ Can be influenced by either high & low performers

★ Typically wants to do a good job and often does

★ Meets expectations regularly

★ Helps to raise awareness of problems but may not have a ready solution(s)

★ Usually follows everyday policies but may push boundaries

★ Is generally committed to making the team a success but needs coaching on the "how"

★ Invested in getting better but needs coaching

★ Usually communicates effectively but can get derailed at times. Occasionally, uses we/they language; can devolve into incivility & disrespect, especially when under pressure or in defense mode

★ Sometimes demonstrates the check list mentality; wants to get an assignment done but it may not be thorough, complete and/or top quality

★ Can settle for "good"

★ Provides some feedback. Accepts constructive feedback but may not seek it out.

★ Misses the big picture in favor of staying in the weeds

★ Can identify next steps with coaching

Red Zone—The Accountability Challenged accounts for 15 – 20 percent of team members on average.

✓ Uneven or poor attendance track record; unexplained absences; clock watcher

✓ Master of we/they thinking & speaking

✓ Passive aggressive at times

✓ Is a sour or toxic presence many times; sometimes "stirs the pot"

✓ Points out problems negatively; sees solution development as someone else's job

✓ Team members tend to avoid him/her

✓ Does the minimum required; looks to "get away" with something or "get by"

✓ Thinks they will outlast the boss or the new policy, etc.

✓ Views "them" as the problem

✓ Takes longer breaks; frequently compares self to others

✓ Little genuine commitment to learn; develops skills only when forced

✓ Gives feedback in a negative way; often defensive when receiving it

✓ Can withhold information

✓ Often stuck in dysfunctional comfort; change resistant

✓ Habit of blame-storming, gossiping and/or complaining

Coaching Questions

In what Zone do you operate most often? What behaviors in the Zone really resonate as signature strengths? What are your growing edges?

_____

_____

_____

_____

In what Zone do individual members of your team perform? For larger teams, document your notes in a separate document.

_____

_____

_____

_____

The insights that we receive from thoughtfully answering these two coaching questions will help us to more accurately select the coaching skills that we'll want to activate in our everyday conversations and aim them more effectively to achieve results more quickly. And that's the name of the game!

As part of his contribution to redefining and re-igniting the spirit of community in our country, Peter Block boldly declares that changing the conversation will change our culture.

Change the conversation...Change the culture.

Peter Block

I believe that the same is true for co-creating widespread accountability across our organizations. If we want a culture punctuated by high levels of personal accountability, then we must start by changing the nature of the adult conversations that we're having with one another (and with ourselves too)! The performance zones can help us to laser focus our coaching message and give us a decent shot at influencing behavior.

I want to share some specific coaching tips for each Performance Zone but before I do, I want to say a word about accountability and self-coaching.

Yep, it's the "You First" talk!

Accountability and Self-Coaching

No matter who you are, what your position is or where you fit in the organization, there are plenty of people who see and/or experience the choices that you make throughout each day. You team knows if you are an accountability hero, even if they don't yet have the language to provide you with that feedback; it might come in disguise as a complement—

> *"You really walk your talk."*
> *"You're true to your word."*
> *"I trust you."*
> *"We can always count on you."*

It's equally true that your colleagues know if you are an accountability zero; a "do what I say, not what I do" person who expects/wants others to act as accountable adults but does little to meet that same standard or selectively exempts themselves from it.

Before you engage in new conversations of accountability with those around you, it's vital that you examine your own behaviors, notice any performance gaps related to accountability and take immediate, visible and swift action to remedy them. You must authentically be able to place yourself in the Role Model Zone by unfailingly demonstrating *green* behaviors most often *or* you must have a specific plan on how you will build and grow yourself and move there quickly.

If, for whatever reason, you find yourself identifying most closely with the *red* behaviors of the Accountability Challenged, stay fanatically focused on your work for now; limit your accountability conversations to those you have with yourself. You can't credibly coach others from your current performance level.

Now, let's aim ourselves at understanding and applying tailored coaching messages for each accountability performance zone. Remember, engaging in coaching conversations is a universal responsibility we all share. No one gets to opt out. And coaching conversations move up, down and across our organizations. That means that each of us will, mostly likely, have such a conversation with our boss, our peers and those who report to us at some point in time. And, finally, we must be open and receptive to be coached by others. If you're scratching your head and wondering what coaching is all about, read/review *Take The Lead: Full Throttle Engagement Powered by Coaching*. I think it will answer most of your questions.

Coaching The Accountability Role Model

Wait a minute! Accountability Role Models don't need coaching! Or do they?

People often think that coaching is reserved for the "screw ups" or those missing the mark somehow. That's wrong-headed thinking. Coaching is an approach that can and should be applied regularly to absolutely *everyone* because it's about helping others to be the best version of themselves and achieving greatness. Coaching is often about the best becoming better! And that's the case with the Role Model. In fact, we should be spending 80 percent of our time, energy and attention on coaching the high performers and high potential performers around us.

Coaching is often about the best becoming better!

What are the **key coaching messages** to share with the Accountability Role Models around you?

✪ **Acknowledgement**—Recognize their contributions in specific detail. Stay focused on accountability. Use what's right framework. Engage in *stay interviews.*

✪ **Appreciation**—Express genuine gratitude for their everyday leadership.

✪ **Plan for Leadership Development**—Understand their preferred career trajectory and actively help them to pursue and achieve it. Ask them how you can best support them and add to their success.

✪ **Ask for the extreme**—Together, co-create one or more stretch goals or assignments that will allow them to play even bigger and become even more influential.

✪ **Reward**—Provide new levels of freedom, responsibility, compensation and/or influence, depending on what they view as valuable.

✪ **Cultivate success partnerships**—Pair an Accountability Role Model with an Accountability Student in a formalized coaching relationship to promote new choices and behaviors on the part of the Student.

✪ **Engage with equal measures of accountability**—Commit to doing what's right for the Role Models among us.

Beware! When it comes to coaching the Accountability Role Model, intentionally avoid the following familiar traps:

★ Taking the Role Model for granted

★ Expecting too much, too soon. Every leadership journey is unique.

★ Not allowing them to lead from their seats

★ Overburdening; burning out these "go to" team
   members

Coaching the Accountability Student

The word *student* says it all! This has all of the potential to be an active learning and growth Zone! New team members are likely to spend some of their on-boarding time in this Zone and that's perfectly reasonable. In organizations where accountability is not embedded in the culture, this will be the Zone with the largest population. Even as we shift our organization's culture and focus increasingly on accountability, there will be those who will take longer to adopt the new behaviors; and those who will need additional coaching. With all of that being said, building and growing the Accountability Student can be some of the most fruitful coaching work that you do and, some of the most rewarding. This is a group with which sparks of possibility can move the Student to higher performance levels and new leadership maturity.

Movement is a key coaching concept with the Accountability Student Zone. The primary coaching message is…

Move up! Grow up! Reach for the behaviors of the Role Model!

In other words, we want the Accountability Student to identify with the Role Model Zone more and more. We want the Student to "grow up"; to grow themselves to the next level of accountability. This is trickier than it may sound. My own qualitative research suggests that the Accountability Student is pretty easily influenced—in both directions! They can either model the choices that role models make OR they can be influenced by the Accountability Challenged. Job #1 as coaches in our organization is to do our part to aim them in the direction of the Green Zone!

---

*"Leadership is lifting a person's vision to high sights;
the raising of a person's performance to a higher standard;
the building of a personality beyond its normal limitations."*
Peter Drucker

What are the **key coaching messages** to share with the Accountability Students around you?

- ✪ **Express belief**—Specifically and frequently communicate your belief in their ability to perform as a role model.

- ✪ **Focus on "what's right"**—Help them to identify their strengths. Point out real examples of role model behavior in real time. Reinforce accountable choices.

- ✪ **Set goals**—Explore their personal vision; help them to create goals that will grow them up to Accountability role Models. Discuss what that would look like and feel like to them.

- ✪ **Schedule regular accountability checkpoints**—Embed the Accountability Credo in the DNA of the Student through intentional repetition, relevant situation analyses and other ongoing learning, formal and informal.

- ✪ **Call out snap backs**—Use "just in time" coaching moments to identify those instances in which the student defaults to less accountable behaviors. Help them to get back on track.

- ✪ **Create formal success partnerships**—Pair an Accountability Role Model with an Accountability Student in a formalized coaching relationship to promote new choices and behaviors on the part of the Student.

- ✪ **Encourage risk taking**—Support bold movement and brave moments when the Student does the right thing, particularly when the right thing isn't the easy or popular thing to do!

- ✪ **Reward**—Find creative ways to acknowledge incremental movement and sustained growth. Paint a picture of power and possibility.

- ✪ **Share the big picture**—Begin to help these colleagues come up out of the weeds for a broader view. Help them to understand the role that they play in the success equation as accountable adults.

"It takes courage to grow up and become who you really are."

e.e. cummings

Warning! When coaching an Accountability Student avoid the following pitfalls that can derail progress:

★ Underestimating the influence that the Accountability Challenged can exert.

★ Settling for the Accountability Student Zone. It is true that some team members may not be fully capable of achieving and sustaining the Role Model level; but many can! Resisting growth is not an option!

★ Assuming that the Students know how to move to the next level. Assisting them in outlining next steps is a must!

Coaching The Accountability Challenged

While 80 percent of your time, energy and attention should be directed toward Role Models and Students, that doesn't mean that the Red Zone - Accountability Challenged are lost causes. I believe in people's ability to change; and I have personally witnessed significant shifts in people—from zero to hero - that others had written off. It will take creativity and resolve on your part; you'll need to be clear-headed and sure footed; and your coaching skills will be tested in new ways. But you can successfully coach these colleagues to achieve a high performance level.

The need for prompt, significant change in attitude and behavior is the coaching theme in the Red Zone. This translates to immediate movement. The Accountability Challenged colleague must move up quickly and notice-ably or they will need to move out, one way or the other. Now, I believe in second chances. After all, no one is perfect; we've all exercised bad judgment on occasion and we've all had bad performance moments. But when this is an ongoing pattern with someone, it's time for a serious adult conversation about the future. If you think this is harsh, think again. Looking the other way or being hyper-tolerant of these habits sends an unmistakable signal to the other team members who are practicing accountability! It can fracture team chemistry and performance; cause Accountability Students to second guess their own behavioral choices and decrease overall engagement levels. Addressing these gaps in accountability is the *right thing to do* for peers and for bosses in particular. Remember, what you permit, you promote!

What are the key coaching conversations to share with the **Accountability Challenged** around you?

- ✪ **Level set expectations and consequences**—Use clear straightforward way messaging to reiterate expected behaviors, attitudes and performance standards along with the consequences for meeting them as well as those for missing the mark on them. Identify the specific time frame for change to occur. Rely on coaching questions and active listening skills to be sure that the message has been understood. For some, it can be important to note that the time for excuses has passed; and no more "get out of jail free" cards will be given.

- ✪ **Review the impact**—Identify the impact that this ongoing pattern is having on the team, your clients and the organization.

- ✪ **Explore resolve**—Using coaching questions, assess the person's determination to turn their behavior around immediately and *permanently*.

- ✪ **Redirect excuses and blame-storming**—Stay focused on the moment. Call out attempts to hijack the conversation by discounting the behavior or alleging that others do the same.

- ✪ **Co-create a plan with specific goals and completion dates**—It must be understood that the goal is not a temporary fix; rather this is about a new, sustained way of being at work.

- ✪ **Express hope**—If it is authentic, share your hope that the person will choose to make the changes. Share the basis for your hope, for example, the person has made some positive contributions in the past or s/he has a unique talent in some area.

- ✪ **Separate the past, present and future**—Remind the person that the past does not necessarily predict the future. They have a choice right now in the present to create a different reality in their future.

- ✪ **Share willingness**—Discuss the specific ways in which you are willing to help this person to improve. For example, brief weekly meetings to check on progress.

✪ **Restore trust**—Identify ways in which your relationship (as a peer or a boss) with the person can improve over time if the person chooses to adopt new habits.

Coaching conversations with the accountability challenged are often tough. Delaying them or avoiding them rarely helps and often is interpreted as permission to continue. But, **what you permit, you promote!** Be on the lookout for these self-sabotaging tendencies:

★ Acting like a parent instead of a peer or a boss. This is not about coaxing, begging or cajoling someone to do the right thing. And it's not about enabling a way of being at work that's just plain wrong. Remember, your colleague is a capable adult who can make different decisions in the future and chart a new direction.

★ Using threatening, one last chance language. Keep your tone of voice charge neutral and straightforward. Stick to the facts. Remember, you must role model accountable behavior even in very difficult circumstances.

★ Allowing fear to prevent you from doing the right thing. As a boss, you may be afraid of losing this person; after all, isn't a warm body better than nobody? Almost universally, the answer is no. The cost of keeping the accountability challenged is really high. And as a peer, you may fear retaliation or isolation for speaking up. More often than not, though, other team members are grateful that you did and remorseful that they too didn't do the right thing and address the issue head on.

★ A case of the guilts—Who am I to address these issues with a colleague? After all, I'm not perfect. No, you're not perfect but you are accountable. As a peer, the right thing to do is to talk directly to the person. Your silence does nothing to help him/her. And, as a boss, it is your duty to have such conversations. The Accountability Challenged have earned such conversations by the ongoing choices that they are making.

★ The path of least resistance—We've acknowledged that coaching around a lack of accountability is hard work that requires perseverance. It places demands on your time and energy. It can wear you down. In fact, that can become a strategy employed by the Accountability Challenged—they believe that they will outlast you and you'll give up, give in and put up with their behavioral choices. Sometimes, it does seem much easier to throw in the towel and tolerate the offending behavior. Weigh the cost to the team and the work and then you decide if it's worth it in the long term.

The Receiving End

This chapter has focused on delivering strong coaching messages to those with whom we work. It's critical that each of us summons up the courage to talk with one another about gaps in accountability. The messages differ dramatically by performance zone because we must meet someone where they are today if we want the conversation to make a difference. But the end goal remains the same regardless: To co-create, enhance and sustain an environment in which we act and are treated as adults; and, as a result, we exceed customers' expectations, enjoy wild success together, look forward to being at work and being memorable in a good way together!

Our conversation wouldn't be complete, however, if we didn't consider what it takes to receive accountability-specific feedback from someone important to us—a boss or a peer, or perhaps a brave direct report. We all need to get right with receiving input and insights from others. The following list of self-coaching suggestions can truly be game changers if you earnestly put them into practice.

Game Changing Tactics for Receiving Accountability Related Feedback:

✪ **Expect it**—Feedback is a universal tool for building and growing yourself and others. Open yourself to the considerable upside of feedback. Be receptive. In fact, get out ahead of it and ASK for feedback. It's change done by you, not to you and that feels very different to many of us. Prepare ahead of time by imagining such an exchange; through journaling or role play.

✪ **Assume good intentions**—Give the other person the benefit of the doubt and think the best of their motive for initiating a conversation. What if they are trying to help you? What if they have a point?

✪ **Avoid a rush to judgment**—Muster your best listening skills and hear the other person out while…(get ready for it) suspending judgment on their message. Manage your fight or flight reflex. Avoid the need to defend yourself. Listen. Ask questions. Think about what you heard. Then respond.

✪ **Tame your ego!**—Acknowledge the possibility of blind spots. There's a good chance that the other person has a valid point. Many times, we have blind spots when it comes to our behaviors and their consequences. Too often we are on autopilot and it feels as though it's the right thing to do only because we've done it countless other times. Your behavior may feel familiar but that doesn't make it "right."

✪ **Look out for mind tricks**—Try to remain as objective as possible as you assess the feedback. Your inner gremlin will work hard to compel you to find reasons to reject or discount the accountability message. Your inner coach will force you to deal with the unvarnished truth, even if it stings a bit. To whom will you listen? Own your non-accountable behavior and make a different choice by identifying one or two simple straightforward do-ables.

✪ **Vow to be your best**—Put the feedback in the context of self-reflection and self-improvement. If someone's feedback helps you to get out of your own way and be a better person then it's worth it. Be humble.

This chapter has been all about behaving our way to higher levels of accountability and, therefore, performance. Starting with ourselves (self-coaching) and then providing and responding to coaching feedback. The coaching messages that correspond to each Accountability Zone must always be shared with others in ways that are consistent with the legal and administrative policies, processes, contracts and procedures of your organization. After all, doing the right thing means that we too must follow these rules! Two wrongs do not make a right. The way that you go about having such conversations matters. So, no shortcuts!

Accountability TO GO

✪ Find article on feedback to recommend.

✪ Polish your listening skills. Review the section on listening in chapter 6 of *Take The Lead* beginning on page 127.

✪ Use journaling as a tool to help you prepare for the feedback from others.

✪ Ask a colleague to provide you with feedback on your current level of accountability. Schedule that meeting immediately.

✪ Find a willing partner and role play giving and receiving feedback on accountability. Debrief with one another. Find another partner and repeat the process. Need more specific language to boost your confidence? Check out the next chapter and then dive into this assignment.

✪ Go back and review the potential pitfalls associated with coaching in each Performance Zone. Select one that resonates with you and make some notes on how you can avoid it in upcoming accountability conversations.

✪ Lead from your seat and develop an express learning experience (ten to twenty minutes) for your team. Create a familiar scenario and an accountability conversation to accompany it. Deliver it at a staff meeting.

Are you ready to take the next step and experience some examples of everyday accountability conversations? I believe you are!! Let's continue to refine your delivery by embracing new language to go with your new accountability mindset.

10

The Upgrade: Embracing the New Vocabulary of Accountability

"Words are free. It's how you use them that may cost you."

KushandWizdom

"No matter what anybody tells you, words and ideas can change the world."

John Keating

Change your culture one conversation at a time! In *Take the Lead*, I state emphatically that "coaching is a directed conversation that happens all the time, every day, and has purpose and structure....Coaching is thoughtful conversation purposefully focused on bringing out the best in oneself and in others to achieve meaningful goals."

Language is the conduit for change, and the way we communicate with each other will either move us toward or move us away from an accountability-rich culture. Purposefully choose a new and improved vocabulary, including your self-talk, and your behavior will follow. And in that way, you will effectively influence others to do the same. Remember, communication is part of your super-power!

Now is the moment to ask ourselves the all-powerful question: How badly do you want things to improve at work? Because, to permanently re-work something as personal and as deeply embedded as our everyday language, we're going to have to want it badly! Badly enough that we're willing to push through our own knee jerk reaction to cling to what we say today. Badly enough to find our very own calm, steady voice and take the risk of speaking up for what's right. Badly enough to put it all on the line and challenge our colleagues and even our bosses.

Let's look back at the examples of today's everyday accountability conversations that teed up the first chapter in Part Two:

Today's Accountability Conversations:

> *"Who's supposed to be accountable for this?"*
>
> *"You have to do a better job of holding her accountable!"*
>
> *"No one's being accountable"*
>
> *"We've got to hold each other accountable"*
>
> *"Why am I the only one following through on our commitments?"*
>
> *"This is good enough."*
>
> *"That's not my job."*

"Words send signals."

Koozes & Posner

What will tomorrow's accountability conversations sound like? That's entirely up to each of us! Here are some examples of a new brand of accountability vocabulary that would inspire me to achieve a higher leadership orbit:

Tomorrow's Accountability Conversations

"I own that part of our work."

"We see each other and treat each other as capable adults here."

"I need to speak up about what just happened. It wasn't the right way to treat a team member and we need to make it right."

"That's cheating and I'm not going to be part of it."

"I'm sorry I'm late. No excuses. It won't happen again."

"What can I do to help you hold yourself accountable for your commitments?"

"I made a mistake and here's how I'm going to make it right."

"There was no excuse for the way that I acted yesterday. I apologize."

What would you love to hear more of at work? What would be an exciting signal that you and your colleagues are on track for a fairer, more adult, more accountable environment? Take a moment to write down your thoughts:

_____

_____

_____

_____

If you're already hearing more of these types of conversations around you at work, then take a bow and celebrate…and then do all that you can to increase the frequency and make them more widespread.

If, on the other hand, you're thinking, "…when pigs fly," then drop the cynicism (so not accountable!) and lead from your seat, doing all that you can to influence the vocabulary. At the risk of being repetitive, I once again challenge you to reject the self-talk that tells you "things and people won't or can't change; that it can't or won't happen here; that we should just accept it as the way things are because it's been that way forever or that one person has no power to make a difference." This reminds me of a famous quote by Ann Bradford, "Tell the negative committee that meets inside your head to sit down and shut up."

"Tell the negative committee that meets inside your head to sit down and shut up."

Ann Bradford

In their book, *The Leadership Challenge*, Koozes and Posner offer elegant support for developing a more intentional leadership vocabulary. They say, "One route to a true and genuine voice is in being more conscious about the words you choose and the words that you use. Words matter. They're as much a form of expression for leaders as they are for poets, singers and writers. Words send signals."[17]

Here is a place to begin. To promote and then support an ever present focus on accountability, upgrade your vocabulary to include more of these twenty words or short phrases:

The Upgrade

- ✪ Do the right thing
- ✪ Hold myself/ourselves accountable
- ✪ Own it
- ✪ Ownership
- ✪ Own the moment!
- ✪ Capable adult(s)
- ✪ Own your work/practice
- ✪ Help others to hold themselves accountable

---

17   Kouzes, James M. and Barry Z. Posner. *The Leadership Challenge*. San Francisco, California: John Wiley & Sons, Inc, 2007. Print.

✪ Choice/Choose

✪ Purposeful/Intentional

✪ I'm personally accountable

✪ Own up to your/our mistakes

✪ I've got this

✪ What you/we permit, you/we promote

✪ I'm leading from my seat

✪ Challenge "same-old same-old" thinking

✪ Accountability role model

✪ This habit is short circuiting accountability

✪ This is an accountability-rich culture!

✪ I am accountable for the success of this organization

And while you're at it, here's a bonus list of words or phrases that we should seriously considering retiring from our workplace vocabulary:

★ Mom, dad, mother, father, parent

★ Children or kids

★ Hold others accountable

★ Who's to blame?

★ Blame-storming

★ It's not in my job description

★ That's not my client/customer/patient

While it's important to demonstrate leadership and do our own self-improvement work first, our responsibility doesn't end with upgrading our own vocabulary. At some point we will need to have a "conversation of accountability" with a colleague about their choice of behavior or attitude. It's not "if it will happen," it's "when it will happen." That's because as adults, we share a responsibility for our culture. This is not exclusively the responsibility of our manager or the human resource team. They aren't present for every interaction or conversation.

Sooner or later, you are going to be the one who hears or sees something that contradicts the Accountability Credo and the culture of accountability that we are building together. And as a colleague and a capable adult, you will need to confront that behavior or attitude in real time, as it's happening if we want to tip the odds in favor of an accountability-rich culture. Remember, research tells us that the most powerful type of feedback is peer to peer. You have enormous influence in these moments and you need to "own" them.

The simple Do's and Don'ts that follow are gentle reminders intended to give you traction as you change the accountability culture one conversation at a time.

Conversations of Accountability	
DO	**DON'T**
Role model accountability	Speak harshly
Be respectful & civil	Use an accusatory tone
Be calm & clear	Use judgmental words
Use a neutral tone of voice	"Gang up"
Ask questions rather than scold	Talk behind anyone's back
Be prepared	Overstate the behavior
Speak privately w/o distractions	Wait too long
Use specific examples	Excuse behavior (that's just her)
Listen clearly & actively	Assume that someone won't change
Encourage the other person	Be afraid
Discuss your choices	Assume that someone else will have the conversation
Remind the person that we are all adults	Say "it's not my job"
Notice & appreciate changes	Use your "Mom" voice or look
Tell your story	Condescend or act "holier than thou"
Talk to your boss/coach if you need support	

Applying The Upgrade

It's one thing to read about a new skill and intellectually understand it and quite another to practically apply it to everyday interactions and conversations. Both are important, but I think you know which of those two is our ultimate end game. We can't stop after we review something new and think we'll master it through osmosis. Or believe that it will be a slam dunk, coming naturally to us. In order to create a new habit that replaces an old, familiar one, we must break with the old and breakthrough the awkwardness and discomfort of the new.

Now's the time to apply your very own communication upgrade and transform everyday conversations at work by infusing them with the new vocabulary of accountability. The best way to do that is using role play and situation analysis (No eye rolling or groaning allowed! They may not be your favorite thing but they're effective!)

Let's practice having a new brand of accountability conversations using all too familiar situations that occur in workplaces everywhere! We'll complete the first one together to get some traction. Then you complete the remainder on your own or as a team exercise. These situations can easily be worked into a mini in-service program, brown bag lunch topic or agenda item for your staff meeting to build skills together as a team.

Situation #1

A Desk Clerk at a busy urban hospital answers the buzzer at the nurses' station and learns that a patient wants to use the bathroom and needs assistance. He pages the Nurse assigned to the patient that day, who responds quickly, stating that she is busy caring for another patient. She asks that the desk clerk page the nurse aide instead. The nurse aide is paged and is also busy assisting yet another patient. She will be free in about 15 to 20 minutes. Three other nurses are sitting at the station completing important charting documentation and listening to the Desk Clerk's conversations. None of them offer to assist.

The desk clerk begins to feel frustration creeping into her thoughts and her body language. He decides to ask the three nurses at the desk for help. His request is met with "it's not my patient" from all three as they leave the area. The desk clerk is now fuming. And the patient still needs immediate help.

Situation Analysis—In a healthcare setting, it's all about delivering high quality care and an excellent experience to every patient (customer). It's the top priority! *Every* member of the team shares the adult responsibility of making that happen. Yes, the care of patients on each Unit of a hospital is typically divided among the health care team on a given shift. But that does not diminish or eliminate every team member's personal accountability for the well-being of ALL patients entrusted to their care. While the patient may not have been formally assigned that day to any of the three nurses at the desk, that patient is still *"their patient"*. Their colleague is busy helping another patient; **the right thing to do** is for one nurse to interrupt his/her charting to help the patient to the bathroom.

The "Same-Old Same-Old" Conversation—In organizations where accountability isn't an embedded cultural habit, it's unlikely that the Desk Clerk will talk directly to the three nurses about the situation. Often the clerk will have had no education on how to have such conversations of accountability. There is also a difference in rank. In a traditional organizational structure, the clerk may not see it as his place to speak up and confront the behavior. Or, there may be fear about overstepping boundaries or even retaliation.

So, often what happens is that the desk clerk angrily complains about what happened to everyone but the three nurses. The level of frustration remains high and unresolved. Trust will erode between the clerk and the three nurses. Opinions, right or wrong, will be formed. More people are drawn into the circle of gossip. We're locked in a vicious cycle.

Sometimes, the clerk will report the incident, after the fact, to a supervisor or manager. That conversation often ends with, "*You* need to talk to those three nurses and tell them that their behavior was unacceptable! But don't tell them that I was the one who reported them. I don't want any trouble and I don't want them to be mad at me." Speaking with your boss can be a legitimate way of taking action. But insisting that your feedback remain anonymous puts your boss in a tough spot and may limit her/his ability to address the behavior and resolve the situation once and for all. In that case, the boss's conversation with the nurses will most likely begin with…"It's been brought to my attention that…" And almost universally, the next question from the other person(s) will be, "Who told you that?" Again, this path often leads nowhere; another vicious cycle. (Note: An exception would be in cases in which the threat of retaliation is significant and very real.)

Accountability Conversation

Instead of a vicious cycle, adult conversations of accountability have the potential to create a virtuous cycle. In this situation, I see two parts to the conversation:

Part 1: When the clerk's initial request is met with the "not my patient" comment, he could summon up the courage to immediately approach the three nurses and, with a calm, non-judgmental tone of voice specifically address the urgent need to take care of the patient's request:

> *"If our patient has to wait for Sue (the nurse assigned to that patient that day) to be available it's going to be another fifteen to twenty minutes, maybe longer. That's not an acceptable level of care. And besides, we own the well-being of all patients on the Unit. The right thing to do is to jump in and help; that means that one of you must take the patient to the bathroom and be sure everything is okay. Who's in the best position to do this?"* (A thirty second conversation!)

Part 2: Once the immediate patient need is handled, the clerk may choose to follow-up individually with each of the three nurses for a more detailed conversation. Here are some options for delivering a message of accountability:

> *"Heather, I'd like to talk to you about what happened earlier with the Sue's patient. It won't take more than ten minutes. What's a good time for you this afternoon?"*

> *"I was surprised by your reaction when I asked you and the other two nurses to help the patient to the bathroom because Sue was occupied with a critically ill patient. I see each of us as being personally accountable for all of the patients here. How do you see things?"*

> *"Can you help me to understand how your response to my request was consistent with our commitment to our organizational value of accountability?"*

> *"What, if anything, could I have done differently to change your initial response?"*

"If you had it to do over again, would you make a different choice?"

"In the future, how are we going to practice what we often say...We're all in this together?"

Now, it's your turn. Read and carefully consider each situation. Write a brief analysis of the situation. In other words, jot down your perceptions & interpretations. Next, imagine the dialogue in an "accountability-challenged" organization. Finally, write a script on how you would deliver a message of accountability in this situation. Use what you've learned so far, and, at the same time, be authentic; use your own words!

Situation #2

A night shift co-worker has a history of sleeping during work hours. Sometimes he nods off in his chair and other times, he finds an out of the way spot in the manufacturing plant to take an extended, undisturbed snooze. This behavior is well known to his team members as well as those who follow him on the next shift. The behavior has also been witnessed by a supervisor at least once. Others must do more than their fair share of the work in order to meet the night's production goals. It is the "elephant in the room" and no one has yet to confront the situation when it is occurring. How can this employee's co-workers handle the situation?

Situation Analysis

_____

_____

_____

_____

_____

_____

The "Same-Old Same-Old" Conversation

_____

_____

_____

_____

_____

_____

Accountability Conversation

_____

_____

_____

_____

_____

_____

Situation #3

For the past four months, a fellow project analyst has been making a very large number of copies for her twelve-year-old son's school projects. It seemed harmless at first but now it feels as though it's the wrong thing to do. She only does the copying when your manager is not present. And she confides in you that she feels entitled to use the machine, paper, ink, etc.

because she has been working long hours on a high profile project. Many other departments have a system to track usage; yours does not because you all agreed to follow the honor system and act as accountable, trustworthy adults. How do you handle the situation?

Situation Analysis

_____

_____

_____

_____

_____

_____

The "Same-Old Same-Old" Conversation

_____

_____

_____

_____

_____

_____

Accountability Conversation

_____

_____

_____

_____

_____

_____

Now it's your turn to identify a specific situation with which you're confronted:

Situation #4

_____

_____

_____

_____

_____

_____

Situation Analysis

_____

_____

_____

_____

_____

_____

The "Same-Old Same-Old" Conversation

_____

_____

_____

_____

_____

_____

Accountability Conversation

_____

_____

_____

_____

_____

_____

_____

Accountability TO GO

✪ Use the scenario that you developed (above) as a mini in-service program at your next staff meeting. Allow your colleagues to work through it on their own and notice how they perceive it and compare their conversation of accountability to the one that you developed.

✪ Add more words or short phrases to the upgraded accountability vocabulary list. Share the list with your colleagues and ask them to do the same. Then count the number of times each day that you use the new vocabulary in everyday interactions.

✪ Add more words or short phrases to the list of vocabulary words that should be retired. Be a role model by deleting them from your everyday conversations. Check with yourself at the end of the day to determine how successful you were.

11

Accountability Partnership: Delegation That Delivers!

"If you want something done right, be an outstanding delegator."

Linda Eve Diamond

"You don't have to do everything!
Even Batman had Robin."

From Poster

If you're considering skipping this chapter because you have no direct reports to whom to delegate, then think again! This chapter applies to absolutely everyone and is an essential link in the chain of accountability that binds your entire organization together.

If you head up a team, unit or department then you will frequently delegate work to others. And, most likely you will receive delegated assignments from others in the organization; either your boss or cross-functionally. If you're a team member, you can expect to receive delegated assignments on a regular basis; and you need to play your role well if there's to be a successful outcome. If you lead a committee you'll be delegating assignments to peers and potentially to your boss! And if none of these experiences apply to you today, there is a strong probability that they will in the future; so build your skillfulness now.

Regardless of their level in their organization, the very best coach leaders who I know made it their business to become highly effective delegators. They really got to know their team members and colleagues well; worked continuously to strengthen trusting relationships; helped others to be the best versions of themselves; and were able to let go and allow others to use their best qualities to complete tasks and accomplish goals.

Effectively delegating power, authority and responsibility to others is the hallmark of the coach leader. It allows us to

- ✪ Practice both leadership and followership
- ✪ Very deliberately build and grow the people around us
- ✪ Help others to find their own unique way of making a meaningful contribution
- ✪ Encourage people to lead from their seats through real, practical application
- ✪ Create a smoother, more efficient work flow and use of resources.

Effective delegation is even more of an urgent business imperative today for all of us! Think about it. The sheer volume of work and its increasing complexity makes it impossible to do it solo. And the fluid nature of career paths means that the players change—sometimes frequently. Delegation fosters a strong bench that makes succession transitions smoother.

In order to fully deliver these benefits, the delegation process must be firmly rooted in the Accountability Credo:

As delegators, we must believe that

- ★ Our team is made up of capable adults
- ★ Most people want to do a credible job; learning and growing along the way
- ★ Delegation is an obvious way to help others to "own their work" more fully; and
- ★ We share in the responsibility to foster an accountability culture and actively participate in the accountability chain.

As delegatees, we must

- ★ Act as adults
- ★ Choose personal accountability for the assignment

★ Accept the shared responsibility to foster a culture that allows this to happen seamlessly day in and day out and actively participate in maintaining a strong chain of accountability.

Simply put, effective delegation and accountability are inextricably tied to one another. It's impossible to separate one from the other. Not when we're talking about the healthy, effective brand of delegation. The kind that delivers both the benefits discussed above and impressive results! If we want to practice and then master this brand of delegation that delivers, then we first must frame it as an Accountability Partnership.

The Accountability Partnership of Delegation

Picture this everyday experience: you've just returned to your work space following the monthly team meeting with a fresh assignment. As a coach leader, unless that assignment can be done in two minutes or less (yes, I really mean two minutes!), you're going to begin to consider delegating it to someone else.

Depending on the size, complexity, nature and timing of the work, this evaluation process could take a matter of minutes or up to a few days. Once the baton is actually passed to someone else, we shift into coaching and teaching mode (followership) and the new owner of the work takes the lead. When the work is complete, we take a look in the rear view mirror to evaluate how well we did.

Or, consider this scenario: The person to whom you report has scheduled a meeting with you to discuss a new project that was recently assigned to your department. You're pretty sure that he wants you to take the lead. You already have a full (maybe even overflowing?) plate and the pressure is already on to get it all done. You're apprehensive about the meeting. On the other hand, the project could give you company-wide visibility and be an opportunity to learn more about a new venture the company is undertaking. It's critically important to understand everything about the assignment before beginning the work. And once you roll up your sleeves and dig into the tasks, you need to know that your leader is going to be there with you and for you throughout the project's life span. You must prepare yourself to confidently ask powerful coaching questions and negotiate the resources and support that you need to be successful. And you definitely want the experience to be a rich source of learning for you; so you'll be debriefing at the conclusion to highlight those lessons learned.

When we slow down the rhythm of delegation—the artful process of entrusting work to someone so that s/he can act for you and the team—three distinct stages come into focus:

- ✪ Delegation Affirmation
- ✪ Delegation Collaboration
- ✪ Delegation Evaluation (Appreciation)

More sophisticated, complex, intense, and/or lengthy assignments will demand more time, energy and attention in each delegation stage.

To get great work done well together, each stage must be infused with a booster shot of accountability. So, let's drill further down into each stage for insights on how to co-create a successful accountability partnership!

Delegation Affirmation

Priority #1 in the initial stage of delegation is for the person who will be delegating the assignment to clearly and thoroughly understand its nature as well as the specific expectations related to it. This search for clarity should include an appreciation for the "why" behind the work.

The delegator then makes the final decision to delegate this work (or not) in the **Affirmation** stage. Once the decision to delegate is made, the delegator shifts to determining the team member best suited for the job and meeting with that person to discuss specifics.

The delegator is personally accountable for:

- ✪ Understanding the nature of the assignment; the reason for it and how it strategically relates to the mission and goals of the organization; and all known expectations, including time frame, description of final deliverable and spending authority.

- ✪ Determining if this assignment should be delegated at all! To make the right call, the delegator should answer the following self-coaching questions:

  - ★ Can this assignment be done in two minutes or less?

★ Is this assignment the best and highest use of my time?

★ Is this an assignment that someone else on the team can do?

★ Does this assignment represent a healthy opportunity for growth and learning for a team member?

★ Am I willing to dedicate the time, energy and attention it will take to delegate effectively?

✪ Selecting the team member who is the best fit for the assignment. (Assuming that the best course of action is delegation)

✪ Facilitating a coaching conversation with that team member that focuses on sharing all relevant details in such a way that s/he gets the whole picture. This dialogue should include but not be limited to:

★ The "why" behind the assignment

★ A clear understanding of the actual deliverable

★ The reasons that the team member was selected for the assignment

★ An agreed upon time frame

★ The available budget

★ The scope of authority, particularly for decision making

✪ Listening carefully to the team members' questions & concerns

✪ Arranging for the necessary resources to get the job done well

✪ Clearly communicating verbally & in writing the agreed upon assignment details

✪ Establishing regular checkpoints for progress updates and trouble shooting

The team member is personally accountable for:

✪ Approaching the assignment with openness and a winning attitude

✪ Bravely asking questions to promote full understanding

✪ Expressing concerns in a constructive way

- ✪ Demonstrating a spirit of cooperation & a desire to do one's part for the team
- ✪ Exhibiting a willingness to take a risk with something unfamiliar
- ✪ Identifying the resources needed to have a successful outcome
- ✪ Negotiating the assignment details to fit current workload

Delegation Collaboration

Delegation is *not* abdication! There is a danger that once we delegate an assignment, we mentally check it off our list and consider it done. Ditch the check list mentality! Anyone who has ever delegated work only to be shocked or disappointed at the end product can testify that this is a rookie mistake that you want to avoid. Ditto, for the person who has been delegated work, and followed through earnestly only to find that there was a serious misunderstanding of the look and feel of the final product!

So, it's broken record time because it can't be said enough:

There is a shared accountability that remains throughout the delegation process!

In the second stage of delegation, the delegator shifts into full partnership mode—coaching, teaching, challenging, supporting and, to an extent, letting go. The coaching checkpoints that were scheduled in the Delegation Affirmation stage serve as milestone meetings for collaboration and connection. For the delegator these are intentional opportunities to build and grow the team member, acknowledge progress, assist in making mid-course corrections and problem solve together instead of bursts of micro-managing mania.

For the team member, the coaching checkpoints represent "lead from your seat" moments. As the person now closest to the actual work, preparing for and leading these meetings falls to you. It's the perfect time for focusing on what's right/working (no harm in engaging in a bit of self-promotion here as well!). Fearlessly ask for what you need: guidance, resources, an objective review of progress, help in clearing roadblocks, etc.

In the **Delegation Collaboration** stage, the delegator is personally accountable for:

✪ Treating the coaching checkpoints as sacred time; only a true emergency would cause this meeting of the minds to be cancelled or rescheduled!

✪ Staying fanatically focused on the assignment. And no multi-tasking, please. Be fully present in the moment

✪ Knowing when to jump in and take the lead and when to remain in the role of faithful follower

✪ Reassuring the team member that his/her full support is unswerving

✪ Helping to navigate around organizational land mines and moderating the level of stress experienced during the assignment

✪ Asking provocative, probing coaching questions that stimulates thinking and may improve the quality of the end product

✪ Acknowledging fine work and creativity and affirming progress

✪ Offering options to assist in navigating roadblocks and obstacles to progress

✪ Clearly identifying if the team member has strayed off course

✪ Collaborating to determine any mid-course corrections that are necessary

✪ Avoiding the reverse delegation syndrome! You know, the temptation to take an assignment back rather than coach through the experience for performance improvement and growth

✪ Settling for nothing less than a great final product

In the **Delegation Collaboration** stage, the team member is personally accountable for:

★ Showing up as his/her best self

★ Doing the work required to move the assignment forward to completion in stellar fashion. The goal is not simply to git 'r done! It's to have a great outcome.

★ Coming prepared to facilitate each checkpoint meeting with a complete status update, delivered both verbally and in writing for most substantive assignments

★ Sharing the many things that are going well with the work, which includes highlighting the contributions of others

★ Identifying problems (or potential problems) and at least one solution for each of them

★ Full disclosure, revealing the unvarnished truth (no sugar coating or telling the delegator what you think s/he wants to hear)

★ Asking specifically for any help that's needed, for example, if there is a roadblock to progress, what is it exactly that you want your Accountability Partner to do about that? Want her to call her counterpart in IT to move your project up in priority? Clarify direction on a part of the assignment?

★ Creating a no complaining, no whining and no bellyaching experience

★ Intentionally managing his/her emotions, motivations and personal energy

★ Scheduling an unplanned checkpoint meeting when warranted to handle urgent issues instead of waiting for the next planned one

★ Turning in a final product that exceeds expectations in all ways

While all stages are important, the Delegation Collaboration is at the heart of the process; it's where the works takes shape, the assignment unfolds and crosses the finish line and, equally important, the relationship between the Accountability Partners becomes stronger, more trusting and mutually rewarding. Strive for this stage to be an energy gain for those involved, rather than an energy drain!

Let's wrap up our review of the all-star accountability partnership on which successful delegation is built by focusing on the final stage of the process, the **Delegation Evaluation** or **Delegation Appreciation.** Once the work is done, you might be tempted to declare victory (or hurriedly pick up the pieces in rare situations) and move on! Not so fast! Slow down to speed up! If you want to embed accountability in your culture then you can't view this final stage as optional. That would be a genuine missed opportunity because some of the best learning and coaching moments happen right here!

There are some lessons that only gain full clarity when you have a chance to catch your breath, and view an experience through the rear view mirror. As the dual naming suggests, there are two primary goals to be met in this wrap-up stage:

✪ Conducting a broad assessment. That includes assessing the process, work flow, decision making, the fit, communications, resources, the Accountability Partnership and, of course, the final work product.

✪ Sincerely, acknowledging the other person's contributions. Focusing on appreciating what worked or what went right during the assignment. And learning from the experience so that we can be better and different in the future. If you're not exploiting each delegation for learning moments, then you're missing a huge opportunity to create a stronger relationship and improve the future work of your team. This is an incredibly important part of the ownership process, so don't discount it.

It would be too easy to skip this stage in the misguided interest of time or efficiency and move quickly to the next new assignment. This debriefing sets the stage for superior future work products, not to mention that it firmly cements the ownership of the assignment.

Top Tips From Delegation Heavy Hitters

"We spend a lot of time teaching leaders what to do.
We don't spend enough time teaching leaders what to stop."

Peter Drucker

In summary, here are some of the top practices of gifted delegators as they elegantly and skillfully navigate the critical crossroads of accountability and delegation. Done well, they can launch you to a new leadership orbit. Miss the mark and you may find yourself stuck in mediocrity:

No leader is an island!—Doing it solo is not an option. We are tethered together in an interdependent web at work. It is not heroic to attempt to do everything yourself. Whether you have "direct reports" or not, all of us need to perfect the art of working successfully with and through others to get work done.

Delegate, don't abdicate.—Your accountability doesn't end when you delegate an assignment. You continue to play a vital role as coach, teacher, success partner and objective sounding board. Spend time. Touch base. Treat the coaching checkpoints as sacred.

Make "crystal clear" your communication goal—"Communication takes a back seat to the work at hand, even if the work at hand is steered and sometimes derailed by the poor quality of communication."[18] Miscommunication, under communication or no communication will torpedo assignments every time. Slow down to speed up is the mantra of delegation super stars. Take the time to explain, listen, affirm…and then do it all over again! World class communication should be our shared goal. Make the conversation safe enough for those receiving the assignments to ask questions, challenge assumptions and ask for help.

Secure the resources to do the job—Assigning work without giving the person the tools and resources that *they believe they need* is setting them (and the assignment) up for failure. Get an inventory of what's needed in the Delegation Affirmation stage. Consider it a must.

You say "tomayto," I say "tomato"—Fully embrace the idea that there is more than one acceptable way to get anything done. Unless absolutely required for regulatory compliance, steer clear of prescribing the "how." Just because you would do it that way doesn't mean it's the only way or even the best way! This is the beauty of delegation. It offers this opportunity to stretch to a new leadership level. And maybe, just maybe to come up with a brand new best practice or a creative way to get stuff done!

---

18   William Noonan. *Discussing the Undiscussable.* New Jersey: Jossey-Bass, 2007.

Give her/him enough rope—This one is a tip of the hat to one of the best delegators I've ever known; my mentor, Dr. Edmiston. I've lost count of the times he said to me, "I'll give you just enough rope to hang yourself!" (Yeah, I know, it sounds a little creepy.) Delegation is about freedom and risk. For both parties. The delegator is free to handle other assignments that are better and higher uses of their time and energy. And the delegatee is free to make decisions that move the assignment forward. To have it their way. The delegator risks failure; and, in different ways, so does the delegatee. Skilled delegators are masterful at balancing freedom and risk. Allowing the person to travel far out on the limb without ever letting them fall.

Track the handoff—Consider this your bonus tip! Whether you use your own personal (home grown) system or a more sophisticated project tracking program, be sure that you write down the details of each assignment and update your notes as the work progresses. No matter how fine-tuned your memory is, none of us have the band width to keep it all straight. Avoid the possibility of things falling through the cracks or sending mixed messages.

"Lead from the back and help others realize that they are in front."

Nelson Mandela

Accountability TO GO

✪ Challenge your thinking on delegation! Most of us are both delegators and delegatees. And if that's not the case for you today, it will be in the future. Pick a day or two and intentionally notice interactions when "getting work done well with and through others" is the purpose. How many were there? What role did you play? Delegator or delegatee? I have known several highly successful professionals who owe their success in large measure to their artfulness and savvy delegation skills.

✪ The next assignment that you delegate, use the three stages of the Accountability Partnership. Notice what worked well and what wasn't quite right.

- ✪ Report to an excessive micro-manager today? Consider teaching that person how to delegate *by acting as an Accountability Partner when a new assignment is delegated to you.* Perfect the role of delegatee. Your new approach could provoke a new level of trust and a different conversation. The new conversation could provide an opening for you to discuss the stages of delegation and make the case for giving it a try.

- ✪ Select one of the **Top Tips** and work to incorporate it into your repertoire.

PART THREE

Choose Accountability Together!

HIGHLIGHTS

The Look and Feel of a Culture of Accountability

✪ Each of us and all of us must foster and sustain a culture of accountability as a non-negotiable requirement in our organization.

✪ The spirit of accountability is alive and well in organizations when the following are increasingly present:

1. Most people can directly connect their individual work and the decisions they make each day to the overall success of the organization.

2. Most people realize that they must be the eyes, ears and voice of the organization.

3. Most people manage their own morale (energy).

4. Most people choose to "lead from their seats!"

5. Most people "own the moment" and show up as the best version of themselves.

6. Most people know the rules and intentionally choose to follow them, whether there is someone watching or not.

7. Most people extend civility, respect and consideration to colleagues.

8. Most people bravely confront accountability gaps in group settings.

✪ Remember the Accountability mantra—**What you permit, you promote!**

✪ We operate as a chain of accountability. When the majority chooses to habitually do the right thing, our chain is strong and allows us to get truly remarkable things accomplished together. On the other hand, when some don't hold themselves accountable, *the entire collective effort is jeopardized.*

✪ Muster the courage to take both the personal accountability inventory and its organizational counterpart.

Step Up and Be a Coach Leader

✪ Coaching is an intentionally designed system for change based on communication that is results-oriented and stokes passion by removing obstacles to our success. By its very nature it helps create the environment where the everyday leader is able to take charge of his or her area and thrive as a result.

✪ *Coach leadership is a way of interacting with another (or others) that promotes improvement and development. In other words, it brings about or contributes to positive change, primarily* **through the will of the other person(s)** *rather than simply out of obedience to me or you or even "them." Great coach leaders believe wholeheartedly that there is brilliance in everyone and they understand just as wholeheartedly that the primary responsibility of coach leaders is to assist others in accessing their own brilliances, their own answers, and then taking inspired action from there to get the work done well. When practiced more and more universally in an organization, by more and more people at more and more levels, coach leadership is the fuel that powers full-throttle engagement. And this fuel is completely renewable and resides in abundant supply within all of us.*

✪ Coach leaders make a daily commitment to be:
1. Intentional communicators
2. Non-judgmental
3. An ego-tamer
4. Open to new possibilities and options
5. Focused on signature strengths
6. Willing to surrender the need to fix others

7. Willing to surrender the outcome

8. Results oriented, not a results machine

9. The Poster Adult for the Accountability Credo

✪ The **Coach Leader's Starter Kit** includes the following basic behaviors:

1. **Coach Leader Behavior #1:** Faithfully practice engaged, clear listening.

2. **Coach Leader Behavior #2:** Choose words with great care (intentional languaging).

3. **Coach Leader Behavior #3:** Be aware of nonverbal messaging and make sensible choices that help (intentional nonverbal communication).

✪ Take the **Coaching Inventory** to determine your skill level. Mastering these essential behaviors and practicing them faithfully is the key to co-creating an accountability-rich culture.

The Unlearning: Recognizing and Changing Habits That Short Circuit Accountability

We must commit to the sequence of learning—unlearning—relearning as we challenge our current habits and move to higher levels of personal accountability.

The Accountability Ten Most Unwanted List includes the following assumptions, attitudes and/or behaviors:

1. Accountability only rests with those in hierarchical leadership positions

2. Playing the role of parent is an acceptable substitute for leadership

3. Acting like a child is the best response to someone else's parenting dynamic

4. Cynicism

5. The victim mentality

6. Settling for mediocrity

7. Conversations consumed by disappointment

8. Dysfunctional comfort
9. The practice of "opting out"
10. Fear

Performance Matters: Behaving Our Way to Higher Levels of Accountability

Accountability Performance Zones offer a way to sort everyday micro-behaviors that exemplify accountability from those that erode it.

The three Accountability Performance Zones are

1. The Accountability Role Model
2. The Accountability Student
3. The Accountability-challenged

Each of the Zones requires a tailored coaching approach to help others move to improved performance.

We need to be prepared to, not only give accountability specific feedback, but to *receive it*!

Accountability Conversations

✪ Language is the conduit for change, and the way we communicate with each other will either move us toward or move us away from an accountability-rich culture. Purposefully choose a new and improved vocabulary, including your self-talk, and your behavior will follow.

✪ To promote and then support an ever present focus on accountability, upgrade your vocabulary to include more of these twenty words or short phrases:

★ Do the right thing

★ Hold myself/ourselves accountable

★ Own it

★ Ownership

★ Own the moment!

★ Working the Accountability Compass

- ★ Capable adult(s)
- ★ Own your work/practice
- ★ Help others to hold themselves accountable
- ★ Choice/Choose
- ★ Purposeful/Intentional
- ★ I'm personally accountable
- ★ Own up to your/our mistakes
- ★ I've got this
- ★ What you/we permit, you/we promote
- ★ I'm leading from my seat
- ★ Challenge "same-old same-old" thinking
- ★ Accountability role model
- ★ This habit is short circuiting accountability
- ★ This is an accountability-rich culture!

✪ Here's a bonus list of words or phrases that we should seriously considering retiring from our workplace vocabulary:

- ★ Mom, dad, mother, father, parent
- ★ Children or kids
- ★ Hold others accountable
- ★ Who's to blame?
- ★ Blame-storming
- ★ It's not in my job description
- ★ That's not my client/customer/patient

Accountability Partnerships: Delegation That Delivers

✪ Effectively delegating power, authority and responsibility to others is the hallmark of the coach leader.

✪ The delegation process must be firmly rooted in the Accountability Credo.

✪ As delegators, we must believe that

- ★ Our team is made up of capable adults
- ★ Most people want to do a credible job; learning and growing along the way
- ★ Delegation is an obvious way to help others to "own their work" more fully; and
- ★ We share in the responsibility to foster an accountability culture and actively participate in the accountability chain.

✪ As delegatees, we must

- ★ Act as adults
- ★ Choose personal accountability for the assignment
- ★ Accept the shared responsibility to foster a culture that allows this to happen seamlessly day in and day out and actively participate in maintaining a strong chain of accountability.

✪ Effective, artful delegation has three distinct stages:

- ★ Delegation Affirmation
- ★ Delegation Collaboration
- ★ Delegation Evaluation (Appreciation)

✪ In each of the stages, *both delegator and delegatee* has specific behaviors and actions for which they are personally accountable. This is why we refer to the delegation process as an Accountability Partnership.

12

Putting It All Together: Crafting Coaching Conversations Focused on Accountability

We've covered a lot of ground, you and I, as we journeyed together to understand, practice, master and commit to personal accountability at work. And, if you were "all in," you've built skill, confidence and resolve along the way.

It's time to drop that final piece into place and complete the puzzle. This chapter offers several examples of peer-to-peer coaching conversations that focus on accountability; and it also offers each of you the opportunity to create one or more on your own.

All coaching conversations are made better by authenticity. This is particularly true of the high stakes conversations focused on accountability. So, I'm not a fan of "scripts." Too often they come across as forced or artificial—a canned-versation instead of a conversation.

These conversation pathways are built with language that suits me. So, if, as you read each of them, you find yourself thinking…"I would never say anything like that!" don't worry. Rather than viewing them as scripts to repeat verbatim, see them as illustrations of what such a conversation could sound like. Allow them to stimulate your own creative juices; learn from them; borrow from them if a phrase is a fit for you; and use them as a teaching tool. Take the Accountability Challenges that are offered here to gain experience, confidence and poise.

When it comes to actually owning the moment and having such a conversation in the course of your regular work day, trust your intuition and your new accountability mindset and allow your coaching skills to shine through.

....

Scenario #1—Nap Time

Scott works the graveyard shift at a manufacturing plant. There are lots of orders to fill and night shift has an important role to play in meeting goals and deadlines. A co-worker, Gerry, has a history of sleeping for long periods of time in the control room. He's worked at the plant for a very long time and has lots of experience. This behavior has been witnessed by a supervisor on more than one occasion but nothing has changed. Co-workers on other shifts are aware of the behavior and make jokes about it frequently. For Scott and the other team members on night shift, it's no laughing matter; it's a real sore spot. It feels unfair and everyone's frustrated. But no one wants to take action because Gerry is known to have a hot temper and there's fear that Gerry will retaliate if his behavior is addressed.

As a capable adult, Scott decides that the right thing to do is to address this behavior directly with Gerry. He has to admit, there's a chance that he'll blow up at him or, worse, find a way to "pay him back" for saying something. If this attempt fails, Scott plans to talk to the manager (the Supervisors are useless) or the Human Resources Specialist assigned to the department. If nothing changes, Scott's going to move on and start looking for another job.

At the start of the shift…

> **Scott:** Hey, Gerry, can we talk for a few minutes before the shift is in full swing?
>
> **Gerry:** Yeah, what's up?
>
> **Scott:** I'm not sure how to start this conversation with you; and, to be honest, I'm not looking forward to it, but here goes….Gerry, almost every night that you're here, you sleep for one to one-and-a-half hours during the shift. You head to the control room, put your feet up on the desk and fall sound asleep….
>
> **Gerry:** (interrupts, and gets defensive) Oh, come on, that's an exaggeration! Once in a while I shut my eyes on my break, but who

176

doesn't! And it's not every night either. I've been doing this job for a long time and I know what I'm doing.

Scott: (calmly) If that were the case, I wouldn't be talking to you. But it's not. It's almost every night and it's not a few minutes when you take a fifteen-minute break either. And, it's been going on since I got here six months ago. I'm not sure that you realize the impact that your habit has on the rest of us. We're working our butts off to make the numbers for the shift. You're the most senior guy we have on the crew and sometimes we don't even know if we're doing things correctly; but we go ahead and do it because you're not around to help. Speaking for myself, I'm frustrated and resentful. This isn't fair and you are way out of line.

Gerry: (in a challenging tone of voice) So, what are you going to do next? Tell the boss? Rat on me? Who do you think he'll believe? A newbie or the guy who's been here almost thirteen years?

Scott: I don't want to have to talk to the boss, but I haven't ruled it out. I came to you "man to man" to talk this out. I did that out of respect for your seniority and your experience and because that's what I would want someone to do for me. Believe me, having this conversation is not my favorite thing. But this can't continue. I've had it! I'm not doing my job and your job anymore!

Gerry: (calmer; persuasive) You have to chill out, Scott. The work will get done. No one will die if we don't make our goals. And, the supervisors look the other way at stuff like this. Heck, they expect that we'll nod off during shifts. No one's getting hurt. I'll cover for you if you want to take a "siesta."

Scott: (resolute owner's mentality) I know right from wrong, Gerry, and this is wrong. Folks are getting hurt—the rest of the team, including me and the company. We missed our bonus by 2 percent last quarter. That's money out of my pocket that I need for my family.

So, here's my bottom line: If you need to rest your eyes once in a while on the shift, then limit it to break time in the break room. Otherwise, please pitch in and do your fair share to help us to get our work assignment done. We need all hands on deck. So, whattaya say?

Gerry: (surprised) You're serious, aren't you? Why would anyone want to work more than you have to, to get by?

Scott: I'm really serious. Look, I'm no hero but I also don't ever do anything less than my best. I'm not looking to just "get by." And you're not getting paid to sleep. I'm asking for your word that you won't sleep on the job anymore.

Gerry: (pauses to think) You're taking a big risk. I have connections here, you know. Who do you think you are, anyway? Who made you the boss?

Scott: I'm not the boss. I'm a member of your crew. We need you to step up. Will you do it?

Gerry: (softening somewhat, shaking his head, almost respectful) Well, I'll give you credit for one thing—you've got a lot of nerve. Not many people would stand up to me this way. And you're like a dog with a bone …… (mumbles) Maybe I have taken it too far; maybe I've gotten lazy over the past year….

Scott: So, is that a yes? We need you.

Gerry: Okay, okay, you wore me down. Yes. Now, can we go and punch in and get to work?

Notes:

Accountability Challenge: Create Alternate Ending:

Here's a leadership dare for you. Imagine that Gerry didn't see the light and give his word to stop sleeping on the job. Where would the accountability conversation have gone then? Working alone or with your colleagues as a team exercise, continue this communication pathway and create an alternate ending.

....

Scenario #2: Being Nibbled to Death by Ducks

Amy has worked at the same financial institution for five years. She enjoys her work most days and has developed supportive relationships with all of her team mates. She and Jennifer have developed a special bond. They work well together, support each other and really enjoy each other's company inside and outside of the office. In other words, they're friends.

Jennifer joined the organization's mentoring program about a year ago and became certified as a coach/mentor. She works with new team members during their four week on-boarding program to be sure that they solidly understand expectations; are building the necessary skills to be successful; and feel warmly welcomed to the organization and the team. She has mentored three individuals who have gone on to do fine work in the organization. She seems to have a real feel for this kind of work.

That's why it's so hard to understand her behavior toward her newest mentee, Shiane. Over the past two weeks, she's nitpicked everything that this once bubbly, eager Millennial colleague does and says. It seems that nothing the newbie does is right or enough for Jennifer. It's really picky stuff. From Amy's perspective, Shiane got a lot of things right. But, in the past few days, she seems increasingly stressed and disengaged; as though she's lost her spark. And today, at lunch, Jennifer openly complained about her to other team members! The others seemed surprised, shocked even, but said nothing. They rolled their eyes, put their heads down and finished eating their lunch in silence.

The real shame of it all is that the bank has had a hard time keeping talented new associates; it's a regular revolving door here. That's why the mentoring program was created in the first place. It seems increasingly apparent that Jennifer has a blind spot about Shiane and Amy has an uncomfortable feeling that she needs to do something about this sooner rather than later.

After much thought, Amy decides to connect with Shiane for a "pep talk."

Amy: Hey, Shiane, want to take a break with me and get a cup of coffee?

Shiane: No, I can't. I have to finish running and collating the monthly reports by lunch and I'm behind schedule. But thanks for asking.

Amy: Okay, then, just a quick five-minute chat in the break room will have to do. (Goes into the break room and encourages Shiane to join her.) I wanted to tell you that I think you're doing well during on-boarding and to see how you're feeling about your experience here so far.

Shiane: Why? What have you heard?

Amy: Nothing. I see you trying really hard to do the right thing and to do things right. And you're a quick study; you really pick things up easily. I think you're a great addition to the team!

Shiane: Well, I wish everyone felt that way. It feels as though I've been picked on, targeted really, since I arrived in the department. My dad used to call this brand of constant criticism "being nibbled to death by ducks." I think it's more like Chinese water torture. It really wears a person down. I don't think my mentor likes me or my work. I get sick to my stomach just thinking about coming into work. And my confidence is about zero. I feel defeated and I don't think this work is right for me.

Amy: It sounds as though things are really hard for you right now. Everything's new. People expect a lot of you. But it's only been two weeks. Why not give it some more time? I'll help you in any way that I can. I think you have what it takes to be great here. We need people with fresh ideas and good energy. And, I remember that it didn't start really clicking for me until I was here a month!

Shiane: Really? Are you just saying that to make me feel better? And it's nice of you to offer to help me; but isn't that Jennifer's role as my mentor? Shouldn't she be the one to build me up?

Amy: First of all, what I told you is a true story. And, second, everyone on the team is accountable for helping new members to learn the ropes. Not just your mentor. Having said that, you're right to believe that mentors and mentees have a special relationship. That's how the program works best.

Shiane: Maybe you could be my mentor. I'd feel so much better if that were the case!

Amy: Shiane, I'm not certified as a mentor and I'm not part of the program today. But I'm your team mate and that counts too. I'm willing to help; to answer questions; and to have a listening ear. Don't forget that relationships are two way streets. Can you think of anything that might help to get your relationship with Jennifer moving in a new direction?

Shiane: I'm so intimidated by her now that I freeze up and don't do my best when she works with me. Maybe I could prepare my questions ahead of time. And I think being more organized would help too.

Amy: Okay, those are two good ideas. Try them tomorrow and see what happens. It's hard to argue with being more prepared and organized! (First time Amy saw Shiane smile all week.)

Amy may have calmed Shiane a bit and helped her to feel less isolated. That's an important first step. But it will be a short-lived change if Jennifer doesn't change her approach. Amy still feels very uncomfortable about Jennifer's behavior toward Shiane. Now she's the one to get a sick feeling in her stomach because she realizes that she'll need to have a conversation with her friend; and it could be a difficult one. Who knows, it could strain their friendship!?!

Amy: Hey, Jen, can I steal ten minutes of your time?

Jennifer: Yeah, sure, and I've been wanting to check with you about the concert on Thursday.

Amy: Okay, but let's put the concert on the back burner for now. I have to talk to you about something here at work.

Jennifer: Whoa, this sounds serious. What's the matter?

Amy: This is really hard for me, Jen. But I'm noticing an approach that's not typical for you and I'm not sure if you realize what you're doing. And, if it were me, I'd want someone to check it out with me. It's about your relationship with Shiane.

Jennifer: OMG, isn't she annoying! She's so perky and upbeat. And she just doesn't get it. And she's needy; she wants feedback all the time...

Amy: Jen, please stop. This is exactly the behavior about which I wanted to talk. You're complaining about your mentee when you're supposed to be her biggest advocate and her teacher. And it's not like you. And it's definitely not the right thing to do.

Jennifer: Oh, it's just us—I feel safe saying anything to you. I'm just letting off some steam. She frustrates me.

Amy: It's still not right. And for the record, I really like Shiane. She's working hard; she's pleasant and asks great questions. And she's fun too.

Jennifer: She is getting under my skin. She has lots of ideas of how to do things differently. And I developed a lot of these processes so I know that they work well. I just have to put her in her place sometimes; she's too forward.

Amy: Jen, listen to yourself. You're criticizing her for offering creative ideas on how to do things differently. Do you think you're being defensive of our current processes because you created them when you were first hired?

Jennifer: I don't really think so...

Amy: The way that you've been treating Shiane is unfair from where I'm sitting. She deserves a mentor that cares about her and wants her to succeed. And a part of that is listening to her ideas and letting her try some of them; and encouraging her to be her best self. I hope that mentor is you because you're one of the best.

But if it isn't then you need to step aside and allow someone else to work with her during on-boarding.

Jennifer: I can't believe that you saying this to me; you're my best friend at work. It's really hurting my feelings.

Amy: I'm saying this to you because I am your friend and because it's the right thing to do. I didn't want to hurt your feelings and maybe I'm not saying it in the best way…but I couldn't stand by any more and watch Shiane lose her enthusiasm and leave the organization. Please at least think about what I've said, sleep on it and let's talk tomorrow, okay?

Jennifer: Okay (skeptical), we can talk tomorrow. I need time to process all of this. If it were anybody but you saying these things, I'd be really angry. You've never said anything like this to me before.

Amy: I had to work up my courage to have this conversation. That should tell you how strongly I feel about it.

Notes:

_____

_____

_____

_____

_____

_____

_____

Scenario #3—It's No Big Deal. Everybody Does It.

You and Bobby have been friends since high school. Your families spend holidays and vacation together. You've both worked together at the huge call center near your hometown for two years, where you've looked out for one another through the good and the not so good times.

Recently, Bobby has been arriving late to work with no explanation, really. You suspect that he's been partying a little too much since his best friend came back from a military tour of duty overseas. Bobby's boss is noticing it too. She gave him a verbal warning yesterday.

This morning on your way to work, Bobby called you and asked you to punch in for him. He was running late and was afraid that he would be in big trouble if he was tardy two days in a row.

Accountability Challenge: You are one of the main characters in this Scenario! What would you do? What would you say? Create your own communication pathway.

_____

_____

_____

_____

_____

_____

_____

Accountability Challenge: For your final challenge, I dare you to create your own scenario as well as the communication pathway to accompany it. Work alone or as a team, your choice.

_____

_____

_____

_____

_____

_____

Submit it to us at info@vantage-inter.com for a chance to win a prize and have your work published on the Vantage website.

Will you take the dare?

....

Scenario #4—

_____

_____

_____

_____

_____

_____

_____

13

Realistic Optimism &
The Conspiracy of Goodness

The pessimist complains about the wind;
the optimist expects it to change;
the realist adjusts the sails

William Arthur Ward

Congratulations! You've undertaken another hero's journey and successfully captured the prize! In Take the Lead, I talked about the importance of being an action hero: a regular person who leaves their routine behind because there is serious work to be done and they are called upon to do it. That's what I'm asking you to do again here in Own It!

Take the work of personal accountability into your head and heart. Take it seriously. Pledge to be both better and different. Leave your familiar world of work and activate this learning, trusting that it will greatly benefit you and those around you. Find the courage to see things through a new leadership lens and to fiercely confront obstacles.

This is the state of mind that has allowed me and many of my colleagues and clients to truly transform our work lives. I have never seen it fail. The prize here is a deep and abiding sense of professional satisfaction that comes from doing the right thing and the pride you feel when you realize that your

187

new behavioral choices are contributing to the re-formation of your work environment into the kind of place to which you want to come each day.

The past several years have presented me with the extra-ordinary opportunity to speak with thousands of professionals about personal accountability. In large audiences and small groups, across industries and disciplines, generations and culture, I've helped small businesses and large international organizations (and everything in between). But no matter the size or the scope, it is always a group of well-intended, dedicated teammates coming together to co-create accountability-rich environments.

People have had a broad range of initial reactions to the messages and the professional mastery challenges that are now included in this second volume of the Everyday Leadership Series, Own It!. Maybe one or two of these sound familiar to you:

✪ It can't be this simple!

> For some, the simplicity of the Accountability Credo and the definition of accountability seems too good to be true. They look around at their own workplace relationships, the everyday interactions of their team mates, the "leaders" in their organization, and the current level of ownership that is exhibited and it feels as though co-creating an accountability-rich culture should be a much heavier lift; that there should be more suffering involved.

✪ It's impossible!

> On the other end of the continuum are the hard-core skeptics, doubters and cynics. We're too used to being told what and how to do our work. Dysfunctional comfort has us all in its grip and just won't let go. We've been "renters" for so long that it's all we know. And frankly, for some, continuing that behavior is the path of least resistance. After all, who would we blame when things go wrong if we owned the moment!?

> And let's not forget those who believe that accountability is either part of your make-up or not. If you weren't fortunate enough to inherit those accountability genes or you didn't adopt it in your early years, you are just out of luck. There's nothing to be done about it other than accepting your limitations.

Finally, the bleak conspiracy theorists wonder if the move toward more personal accountability isn't a trick to get them to do more work.

✪ The other guy (TOG) needs to change, not me.

One of my personal favorites is the "TOG" (The Other Guy) reaction. I know this one is coming when someone pulls me to the side and lowers their voice to a whisper, as though they're about to share something that's top secret. Here's what that sounds like: "This is such a powerful message, and I am sat you are here to share it with the team! It's really important that (fill in the name of a specific person, team, department, generation or class...anyone but the person talking) is here!!! He/They REALLY need to hear this!! To tell you the truth, they're a mess when it comes to accountability. But I'm nailing it; the poster adult for accountability. No changes needed on my end!!"

✪ This is fluff.

For some, the notion of personal accountability at work lands as either the latest program or gimmick to sweep across the business community or something that requires some new personal equipment—a pair of rose-colored glasses! They look past the action orientation and discipline of personal accountability and narrowly view it as hyper cordiality or hyper correctness.

✪ This needs to come from the top!

In too many organizations, team members view themselves as powerless. They don't see the opportunities hidden in plain sight before them; to do the right thing; to own the moment. They underestimate the impact of making those small new daily choices; held hostage by the traditional mindset that has lulled them into believing that unless something comes from the top of the pyramid it's doomed to fail.

✪ We can do this!

You may be familiar with the saying, "When the student is ready, the teacher appears." (attributed to several sources including Buddha and the theosophy movement). For many individuals and organizations, they are at just the right place in their professional development or their cultural evolution that the message and the call to action of personal accountability is right timed, energizing and even inspiring. The soil has been warmed for it to firmly take root.

✪ We're already on our way!

Finally, for forward thinking individuals and organizations, the message of accountability is aligned with their existing plans, goals and progress and actually accelerates their change process. Acting much like a booster rocket, it allows them to enter a higher leadership orbit quickly.

While I respect all others' perspectives and opinions, some of these reactions seem more like excuses to me. Excuses to remain stuck in mediocrity or rationalizations to avoid the uncomfortableness that comes with change and growth.

One More Powerful Take-Away

At the end of Part Two, I shared a powerful phrase that has come to be very meaningful to me: A Conspiracy of Goodness. If you want a conspiracy theory in which to believe, I recommend this one. It has captured my head, my heart and my imagination. It has created sparks of possibility for me and fueled my determination and commitment to be the best version of myself.

Now to be fully transparent, I am a realistic optimist. This world view has allowed me to be inspired by and motivated to action by a belief that co-creating a conspiracy of goodness is really possible!

In an article for Leadership and Management, Andreas von der Heydt describes realistic optimists in the following terms: "They strongly believe that they make things happen and that they will succeed...they perfectly know that in order to be successful they have to plan well, to access all necessary resources, to stay focused and persistent, to evaluate different options, and to execute in excellence."

She goes on to say that: "Realistic optimists stay positive and upbeat about the future, even—and especially—if and when they recognize the challenges ahead. As such realism and optimism are not diametrically opposed. The contrary is true: They're complementing each other in a very powerful manner!" (Leadership and Management December 16, 2013).

Because I am a realistic optimist...

I believe that it is entirely possible to co-create an accountability-rich organizational culture as more professionals make the adult choice to be personally accountable.

I believe that a deeper understanding and steady use of the Accountability Compass will lead to a more virtuous cycle in our relationships that lends itself to the development of a conspiracy of goodness.

I believe that this work is elegantly simple but not at all easy to do day-in and day-out, one interaction and one decision at a time, because it is not our current habit.

I believe that anyone can choose personal accountability as a core value and a way of life. In other words, anyone can learn to act and make decisions from a place of personal accountability. True, there is no fairy dust or magic wand involved. But skill building, resolve and practice will get you there!

I believe that each of us must take a long look in the leadership mirror and honestly evaluate our level of personal accountability at work. No one is exempt. If you're always focused on "the other guy" you probably have a blind spot about your own behavior.

I believe that building an accountability-rich culture leads to a favorable bottom line and delivers all of the success metrics for which we strive.

Finally, I believe in the power of personal accountability to transform ourselves, our workplace, our communities and our world.

I've had my own moments of truth when I had to decide to do the right thing...or not. And as I look in the rear view mirror, I'm proud to say that I chose to be accountable more often than not. For example,

> *I remember a time early in Vantage International's life cycle, when a client told me that they could not honor our contract. They were experiencing significant (and unexpected) financial difficulties and they asked me to release them from their contractual & financial obligation. Now, make no mistake, they were legally bound to pay us. And we were counting on their business to make our own monthly financial goals. We were a young company, and it was a big deal. It hurt. Even though it was very hard, I knew what the right thing*

to do was. I tore up the contract. All I asked was that they consider re-engaging us as soon as they recovered. In a relatively short period of time, they were back on their feet and we received an even larger, more lucrative engagement! And they encouraged others to use our services as well. I will never forget this lesson.

P.S., Even if there was no happy ending for us, I would have done exactly the same thing again.

As you tackle the challenge of accountability, personally and at work, consider the dynamic duo of realistic optimism and the conspiracy of goodness. Then ask yourself: how good can I really stand it?

About the Author

Leta Beam is one of the most powerful and energetic voices for business transformation in the twenty-first century, sharing her message of full-throttle engagement and leadership from every seat through coaching, teaching, speaking, entertaining, and writing.

Leta is President of Vantage International, a premier leadership and business coaching enterprise, dedicated to serving high performing professionals and organizations using a dynamic, results-oriented coaching system called AdVantage. The AdVantage Coaching System challenges clients to view themselves as powerful forces in their own lives and the lives of their organizations. It offers a unique blend of international thinking and laser-focused action steps that delivers significant bottom-line results.

One of her brilliances is helping others to "get on a roll" and stay there. Whether coaching one-to-one with high performing professionals around the world or one-to-many with professional teams, groups, committees, entire businesses, boards of trustees or broad business audiences. Leta's framework is the same: each of us is a powerful force in our own experience, if we choose to be. In order for us to improve our conditions, then, we must intentionally change, not because we are told to or because someone manages, directs, cajoles, or browbeats us—rather through our own will. Sustainable shifts are intentional and self-induced. Every seat is a power seat!

Not everyone is ready to open the throttle up and put the pedal to the metal. Yet Leta creates a safe space in which others can think about things differently and every voice can be heard. Her infections energy helps those around her to believe that everything is possible and inspires them to more actively engage at work.

Leta works at every level from executives to management to team members, entrepreneurs and small business owners and across different industries and disciplines. Leta partners with companies throughout the world such as AHOLD/Giant Foods, Bassett Healthcare Network, Coldwell Banker, Commonwealth of Pennsylvania, KPMG, Lifespan, Planned Parenthood, Ritchey Engineering, and SYMMCO. (For a full list of clients, please visit www.vantage-inter.com.)

Above all, Leta is recognized for an engaging style and fresh, results-oriented messages. She is the author of numerous articles on healthcare, managed care, and most recently, business coaching, leadership, accountability, personal mastery, and business excellence. In front of both national and international audiences, "Leta...leaves the audience changed." You can really have it all in one presentation! Informational and transformational learning; humor and challenge; sparks of possibility. Leta has been featured in newspaper and journal articles as the "energetic woman who can beat psychosclerosis" (hardening of the attitudes.)

Leta shares a home with her husband, Jim, in Central Pennsylvania that is playfully called, "La La Land." Leta was recognized as one of the "Best 50 Women in Business in PA." She has appeared in the "Portraits of Strength" calendar for Pinnacle Health System in Central PA. She is adjunct faculty at her alma mater, Penn State University, where she designs and delivers leadership curricula. Leta is also an adjunct professor at Saint Francis University, where she offers MBA courses in coaching, creating workplace community and talent planning.

She is a bicyclist, ballroom dancer, exercise enthusiast and, most significantly, a lover of life.

To purchase books, please visit Leta at www.Vantage-inter.com

An Invitation to Connect

*Please consider this Leta Beam's personal invitation
to contact her to explore how she can more fully
support you and your organization as you*

build an accountability-rich culture together!

*Lead from your seat, Be Fully Engaged,
Act as an Owner...Be Fearlessly Accountable!*

Please contact us at Vantage International

717-238-3939
leta@vantage-inter.com

How Good Can You Stand It?

*Please visit www.vantage-inter.com to find special pricing for
this book and the set of* Own It! Building an Accountability-Rich
Culture Together *and* Take the Lead: Full-Throttle Engagement-
Powered by Coaching.

CPSIA information can be obtained
at www.ICGtesting.com
Printed in the USA
LVOW11s1827230417
531887LV00002B/358/P